I0236243

IMAGES
of America

FORT RILEY

IMAGES
of America

FORT RILEY

William McKale and Robert Smith

ARCADIA
PUBLISHING

Copyright © 2003 by William McKale and Robert Smith
ISBN 978-1-5316-1768-4

Published by Arcadia Publishing
Charleston, South Carolina

Library of Congress Catalog Card Number: 2003113033

For all general information contact Arcadia Publishing at:
Telephone 843-853-2070
Fax 843-853-0044
E-mail sales@arcadiapublishing.com
For customer service and orders:
Toll-Free 1-888-313-2665

Visit us on the Internet at www.arcadiapublishing.com

CONTENTS

ACKNOWLEDGMENTS

This pictorial history is the result of the hard work of many individuals. I want to thank and acknowledge Terry Van Meter for his years of dedicated service at this institution. Publication of this book builds upon the work he performed at the U.S. Cavalry Museum over a quarter of a century. I want to thank Steve Ruhnke, Don Rush, Chester Johnson, and Deb Clark of the U.S. Cavalry Museum staff for their cooperation in contributing to the preparation and publication of this book. Their diligence in finding and preparing photographs was instrumental in its completion. Special thanks to Gaylene Childs, Director of the Geary County Museum, for sharing the resources of that institution. I especially want to thank my co-author and collaborator, Robert Smith, for his tireless efforts in helping select and write captions for the photographs. His efforts and commitment were critical to the book's completion. Finally, I want to thank my wife, Elaine, who has supported me through this and many other projects.

-William McKale

In preparing this book, it has become obvious to me that an author depends greatly on a number of good people in helping the writer accomplish the task. This book was no exception. I would like to first thank my wife, Karen, who provided input when solicited and even when it was not solicited. Her criticisms were helpful and constructive, as were her patience and forbearance throughout this entire process. I would also like to thank Alex Schultz, who spent many a long evening helping me sort photographs and placing them in a coherent pattern. Alex also displayed an impressive knowledge in the vagaries of computereze, a process that I am afraid that I will never master. In addition, I wish to thank Patricia Spurrier-Bright, who graciously provided me with time to complete this project. Moreover, Tricia provided me with a wealth of information concerning military traditions and United States Cavalry customs. Finally, I would like to thank William McKale for affording me the opportunity to practice the craft of an historian. Each one of these people provided a critical contribution so that this book could become a reality. Many thanks to everyone.

-Robert J. Smith

INTRODUCTION

Fort Riley's History is One of Serving the Nation

The history of Fort Riley largely corresponds to the ebb and flow of Army mission and appropriations. During the 1850s and the Civil War, the fort served as a staging area from which to project a military presence along overland trails and advancing settlements. As early as the spring of 1866, a cavalry colonel wrote that the frontier had passed the fort by. But he believed the post, because of its size and location, should eventually be used as a training ground for cavalry. During the lean years of the 1870s, when Congress slashed army appropriations and manpower to a minimum, army leaders, such as Generals William T. Sherman and Philip Sheridan, were adamant in their belief that this important piece of property should remain under the military's control.

The establishment of the Cavalry and Light Artillery School in 1892 was a step towards building a professionally trained mounted arm of service. The successor to this school, the Mounted Service School, further refined training of the individual soldier and officer, rather than the regiment. During this same period, Fort Riley was selected as one of the installations to host the first large-scale combined maneuvers between regular and National Guard units. The school and these training exercises underscored the fort's continuing importance.

The entrance of the United States into World War I focused importance on Fort Riley as a site to establish a divisional training center. The result was construction of Camp Funston where the Eighty-Ninth and Tenth Divisions, along with elements of the Ninety-Second Division, trained.

During the inter-war years of the 1920s and 1930s, Fort Riley again resumed its traditional role of being a center for instruction, training, and summer camps. The Cavalry School and its graduates assumed a worldwide reputation. World War II placed unprecedented demands upon the nation's ability to mobilize and train troops. Fort Riley was part of this effort with the construction of facilities at Camp Forsyth for the Cavalry Replacement Training Center, and the rebuilding of Camp Funston for use by armored divisions.

The decade following World War II witnessed continued use of the fort as a center for training and education. The Army General Ground School was created and operated until 1950. This school taught new officers the common courses, such as map reading, company administration, and military law. The fort also operated the Army's only Officers Candidate School. Yet another function of the fort during the Cold War years was operation of the Aggressor School. Similar to the OPFOR concept of today, aggressor cadre provided realistic enemy contact for unit training.

Between 1948 and 1954, the Tenth Infantry Division was stationed at Riley and conducted basic training for new recruits. The service of the Tenth was especially important during the Korean Conflict.

The stationing of the First Infantry Division at Fort Riley in 1955 was a new mission for the post and evidence of its adaptability. Focus continued to be directed on threats to our national interests from overseas. The deployment of troops to Southeast Asia in the mid-1960s again witnessed the fort assuming a role of being able to equip, train, and deploy soldiers to world hot spots. This was further evidenced with deployment of the First Infantry Division and other soldiers from Fort Riley during Operation Desert Shield/Desert Storm in 1990 and 1991.

In the mid-1990s, the First Infantry Division headquarters were transferred to Germany. By the end of the decade, the fort's role as a power projection platform was once again recognized when the Twenty-fourth Infantry Division was reactivated here in 1999.

Fort Riley became "America's Warfighting Center", a base for the mobilization, training, and deployment of soldiers. From Operation Desert Shield/Storm to Operatin Iraqi Freedom, Fort Riley soldiers continue to respond to the nation's call.

Today, the soldiers and military families that come to Fort Riley are a continuing link with the legacy of the past. Their service is in keeping with Fort Riley's tradition of defending our nation and its freedoms.

William McKale
Fort Riley, KS
27 June 2003

One

FRONTIER POST

SIXTEENTH INFANTRY REGIMENT. Troops of the Sixteenth Infantry Regiment, along with the regimental band, prepare for a review, *c.* 1879. Dress parades and reviews brought together the splendor and pageantry of the frontier army. This picture shows the band on the extreme right and a company from the Sixteenth Infantry ready for review. Between 1877 and 1880, three companies of the Sixteenth garrisoned Fort Riley. These troops were under the command of Galusha Pennypacker, a famous Civil War hero, the youngest general officer ever appointed to the army, and the youngest colonel ever to command a regiment.

FORT RILEY 1862. Fort Riley was a frontier outpost during the Civil War that occasionally served as a staging site for projected operations. Such was the case in the spring of 1862 when John Gaddis, Twelfth Wisconsin Infantry, produced this watercolor as he sat on the limestone outcroppings northwest of the Main Post area. This is the earliest known image of Fort Riley and is a view of the Main Post Parade Field from the northwest.

FORT RILEY, KANSAS.

FORT RILEY 1870. By the early 1870s, Fort Riley had developed into a substantial post. Some believed the fort's usefulness was gone, as the frontier had long since passed this post by with the arrival of the railroad in 1866. This lithograph depicts the main post area prior to 1872. The view from the hillside above the Ogden Monument provides a seemingly tranquil scene of a well laid-out garrison situated along the gently flowing Kansas River.

11

FORT RILEY 1866. In the fall of 1866, the Seventh United States Cavalry was organized at Fort Riley under the command of Lieutenant Colonel George Armstrong Custer. At this time, the Quartermaster Department conducted a survey of post buildings that included a photograph of the Main Post area. This is the earliest known photograph of Fort Riley, taken in the fall of that year. The building in the foreground is the post physician's quarters. This building was torn down in the late 1930s.

FORT RILEY 1869. By the summer of 1869, the Seventh Cavalry Regiment had left Fort Riley and batteries of the First and Fourth Artillery Regiment's had taken up residence. On a summer afternoon, a group of officers, their wives, children, and pets participated in a game of croquet on the Cavalry Parade Field. This photograph was taken in front of present-day Quarters 21.

FORT RILEY 1870. This photograph, originally a stereopticon view, is taken from the same general vicinity as the 1866 photo and shows the Main Parade Field. The small, fenced building in the foreground is present-day St. Mary's Chapel. The building on the extreme left is the post hospital, which had a second floor added in 1872 and became post headquarters in 1890.

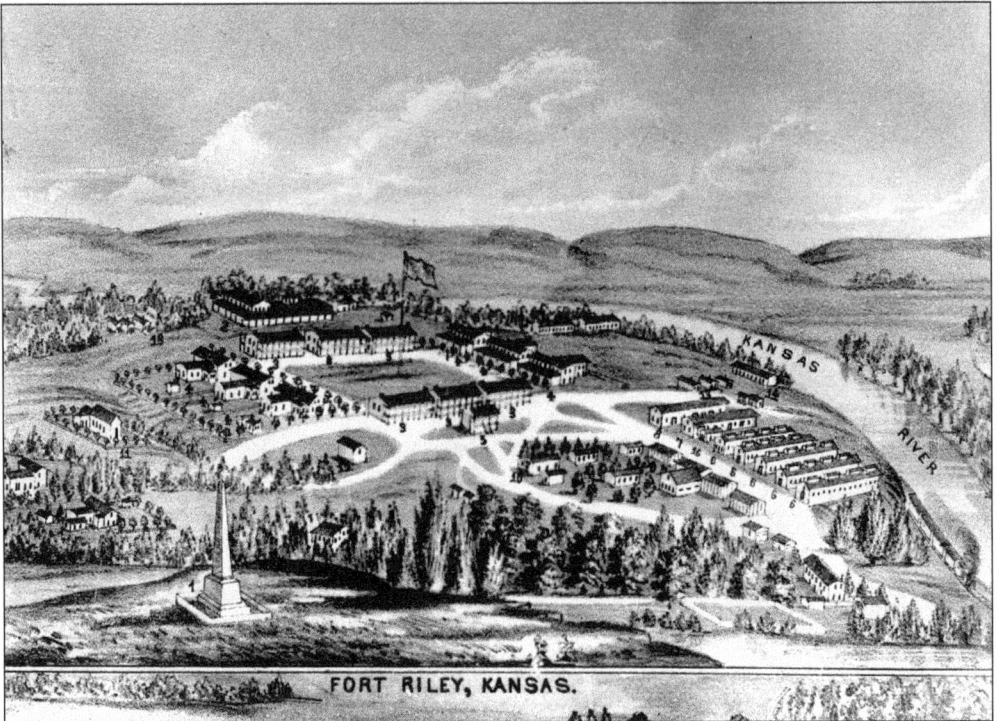

FORT RILEY 1872. This view recaptures the same general perspective of the 1866 photograph.

FORT RILEY LATE 1880s. An actual photograph further documents the evolving nature of Fort Riley in the late 1880s.

CLEANING DAY. The enlisted men's barracks occupied the east and west edge of Fort Riley's Cavalry Parade Field. These two-story limestone buildings were built during a major building boom that began in 1889 and continued into the early part of the 20th century. The group of soldiers gathered in front of their living quarters display a variety of uniforms and equipment. McClellan saddles are placed on wooden horses, grey saddle blankets with yellow woven stripes are hanging on the second floor rail, and two rifle scabbards hang from the second porch column on the left. These soldiers are clad in both issue and non-issue items. The troopers on the far right wear the 1889 drab campaign hat, while a number of other soldiers wear blue forage caps.

SIXTEENTH INFANTRY BAND, c. 1878. In the late 1870s, the Sixteenth Infantry Regimental Band was stationed at Fort Riley. Military bands are an integral part of military life. Bands improve morale by providing stirring music both on the battlefield and at military ceremonies. Garrison commanders welcomed the presence of bands on post, as bands also supplied music for many social events like concerts and balls. Here, the Sixteenth Infantry Band practices on the Cavalry Parade Field.

SMOOTHING CAVALRY PARADE FIELD. In November 1887, work crews with horses and graders began to level and smooth the Cavalry Parade Field. Workers changed the topography of the land by scraping off four to five feet of soil and using the excess soil to fill in ravines. The landscape of the land was altered considerably, as a steep hill in the area was leveled. This conscious effort was an example of the Army's efforts at "domestication of the wilderness" and bringing aesthetic scenery to the plains.

BUFFALO SOLDIER NCO. The Ninth Cavalry Regiment supported the day-to-day activities of the Cavalry and Light Artillery School during the first years of the 20th century. Pictured here are an African-American NCO and his wife during that period.

CAPTAIN LEBO. Captain Thomas C. Lebo of the Tenth Regiment of Cavalry. Lebo served in the Pennsylvania Cavalry during the Civil War. After the war, he joined the regular cavalry and served as a lieutenant on the frontier. It was during this period that the Tenth Cavalry, one of the two famed Buffalo Soldier regiments, completed its formation at Fort Riley. In 1876, Lebo, a captain in the Tenth Cavalry, commanded an expeditionary force of B, E, and K troops that were successful against the Lipan and Kickapoo Indians in the New Mexico and Arizona Territories. This photograph shows Lebo wearing his dress uniform that conformed to the regulations of General Order No. 76, series of 1879. These dress regulations authorized a Prussian looking dress uniform complete with 1881 pattern dress helmet with buffalo hair plume and gilt trimmings.

COMANCHE. In the late 1880s, the Seventh Cavalry Regiment returned to Fort Riley after a twenty year absence. One of the important members of the regiment was Comanche, the Seventh Cavalry survivor of Custer's command at the Battle of the Little Big Horn, was the mount of Captain Myles E. Keough, the commander of I Troop. The gelding was found by the troops of General Alfred Terry standing among the bodies of the slain soldiers. Comanche had sustained seven wounds, three of which were considered severe. The horse was nursed back to health by the cavalrymen and assigned to ceremonial duties. Comanche lived an additional fifteen years after the battle, dying in 1891 at the age of thirty years. He was subsequently preserved and placed on display at the Dyche Museum of Natural History on the campus of the University of Kansas.

LIBBY. Elizabeth (Libby) Bacon Custer was the wife of Lieutenant George Armstrong Custer, the acting commander of the Seventh Cavalry. Just after the Civil War, Custer was assigned to Fort Riley in command of the regiment. Libby joined her husband at the post, occupying the commandant's quarters just north of the Cavalry Parade Field. After her husband's death in 1876, Libby spent the rest of her life preserving his memory. Libby's many books include, *Boots and Saddles*, 1885; *Tenting On the Plains*, 1887; and *Following the Guidon*, 1890. She died in 1933 in Paris, France.

19

THE POST SUTLER. Two views of Moses Waters' Post Exchange in the late 1880s. Moses Waters was born in Ireland and immigrated to America when he was 15 years old. For most of his early life, he was a section boss for the railroad, a buffalo hunter, and an Army scout. As a scout, he served with General George A. Forsyth and took part in battle at Arickaree Fork on the Republican River. In 1875, Waters settled down as Fort Riley's sutler. Waters' two story post exchange consisted of a general store, an enlisted men's bar, a dining room for enlisted men, and an upstairs officers' club complete with dining room, bar, and billiard tables. Waters remained as Fort Riley's sutler until his death in 1889. After his death, his widow sold the building to the United States Government for $5,000.

WOUNDED KNEE MONUMENT. When the Seventh Cavalry Regiment returned to duty at Fort Riley from Pine Ridge, South Dakota, the soldiers of the regiment started a subscription to raise money for a monument for members of the regiment killed at Wounded Knee. About $1,950 was collected, and on July 25, 1893, the monument was dedicated with 5,500 people in attendance. Today, the stone edifice is located near Waters Hall.

ST. MARY'S CHURCH. The Post Chaplain, standing in the church doorway, was responsible for conducting educational classes for children on post. Classes were held at the chapel—today's St. Mary's Chapel—and usually taught by the chaplain or one of his assistants. Pictured here is a group of school children on recess from their studies.

880. Fort Riley.

OFFICERS' QUARTERS. Servants would often accompany Army families to frontier postings. They performed various chores in supporting the day-to-day family life. Pictured in this 1880 photograph (bottom) is a servant who is watching over several children at play. This particular set of quarters is probably the present-day Custer House, located on the north side of the Cavalry Parade Ground. The photo above (top) is another set of quarters. Note a small child standing on the porch.

Two

The Golden Years of a Cavalry Post
1885–1916

Sports and Clowning Around. Sports were popular outlets for soldiers' energies. Here, a group of soldiers practice their boxing skills while a hospital steward looks on with a towel in hand. Other medical personnel look on, one of the spectators in the background may have been a patient from the hospital.

POST HEADQUARTERS. In 1890, Fort Riley's Hospital became the Post Headquarters. A new post hospital was planned and constructed during General Philip Sheridan's 1887 building program that greatly increased the size of the post. The new hospital was built at a cost of $300,000 was completed two years later. This building is located at the eastern end of the Cavalry Parade Field and today serves as the United States Cavalry Museum.

SHERIDAN STREET. Sheridan Street in the early 20th century. In the first decade of the century, Sheridan Street was still unpaved. Note the stone slab hitching post located in front of the fire hydrant. The homes on the left side of the street housed officers and their families. On the right at the far end of the street is the post hospital that today houses the United States Cavalry Museum.

FORT RILEY HOSPITAL. Medical care for soldiers was an important part of morale. The quick evacuation of combat wounded was a critical factor in saving lives. The horse-drawn ambulances fulfilled this need. The ambulance, however, was not solely limited to transporting combat wounded. Officers often used these vehicles to move their families and possessions from one post to another. These vehicles continued to be used until World War I when motorized ambulances replaced the horse drawn ones. This particular horse-drawn vehicle is pictured outside of Fort Riley's post hospital, which was built in the late 1880s and was located northeast of the Artillery Parade Field.

AMBULANCE. This ambulance is outfitted for officers' personal use. Many Army ambulances were also used to transport children to and from the post school.

ARTILLERY ADMINISTRATION BUILDING. During the 1880s, the Commander of the Army, General Philip Sheridan, decided to expand Fort Riley to include facilities for the training of cavalry and artillery soldiers and officers. On the west side of the Artillery Parade Field stood the Artillery Administration building with its distinctive fortress style tower. This picture, taken in the early 1900s, shows a bugler sounding one of the many bugle calls that regulate a soldier's day.

BUGLERS CLASS OF INSTRUCTION. The bugle regulated the daily activities of the soldier from morning to night, or, in the soldier's terminology, from reveille to tattoo. A school for trumpeters and buglers was established at Fort Riley in 1903. Here, one of the first graduating classes from that school is posing with their instruments.

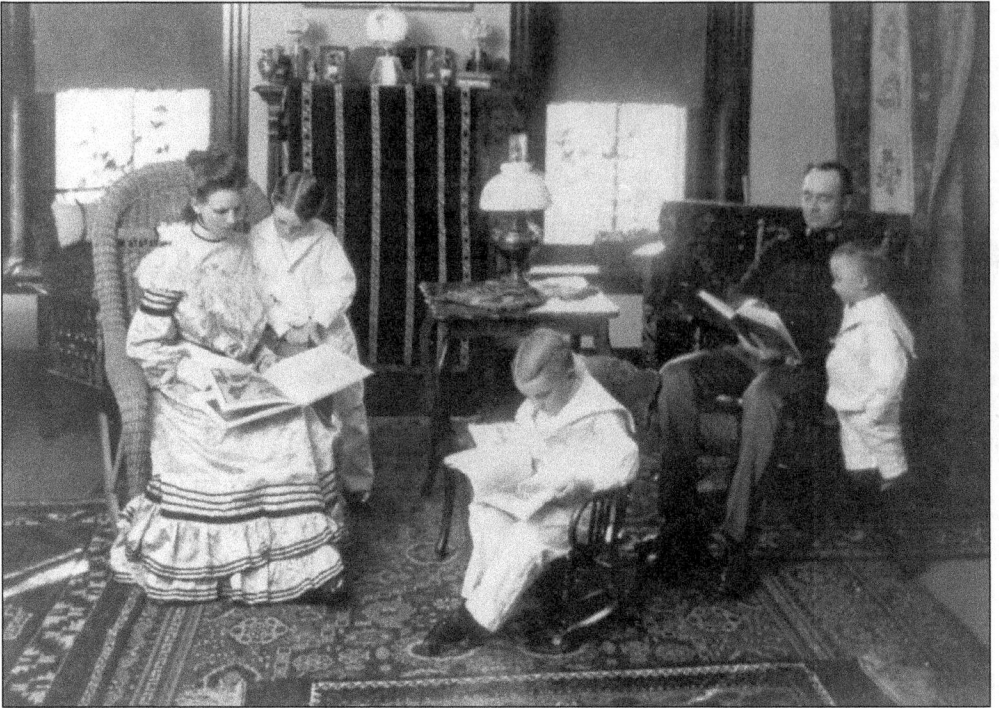

FAMILY PORTRAIT. The establishment of the Cavalry and Light Artillery School in 1892 also witnessed the building of family housing units for the officers that were students on Sheridan Street and Forsyth Avenue as well as Schofield Circle. These stone structures provided comfortable living space for families. This family portrait shows an officer and his family relaxing in the parlor.

CHILDREN'S PARTY. Children dressed for a birthday party on the porch of an officer's quarters in the 1890s. Military children, who were billeted on army posts, were "born into the regiment," which meant that they were inculcated in the military lifestyle. Both officers and enlisted men taught the children to walk and talk the Army way. When families returned to civilian life there was often a period of adjustment for the children as well as for the adults.

FEEDING HORSES. Horses are fragile creatures—even though they have great stamina, they are subject to a variety of maladies. Moreover, active cavalry horses require both grain and forage to carry a trooper, his kit, and saddle. This picture, taken in 1910, depicts artillerymen pitching hay, while the picket lines of horses are eating grain from feedbags. Beginning in 1880, a large portion of Fort Riley's acreage was utilized specifically for hay production. Hay produced at the fort was subsequently shipped to cavalry posts throughout the west.

TARGET PRACTICE. Knowing how to properly shoot a weapon was basic to the military profession. Practice in weaponry involved going to the ranges to hone this skill. Pictured here is a group of cavalry troopers who are taking a break from their target practice.

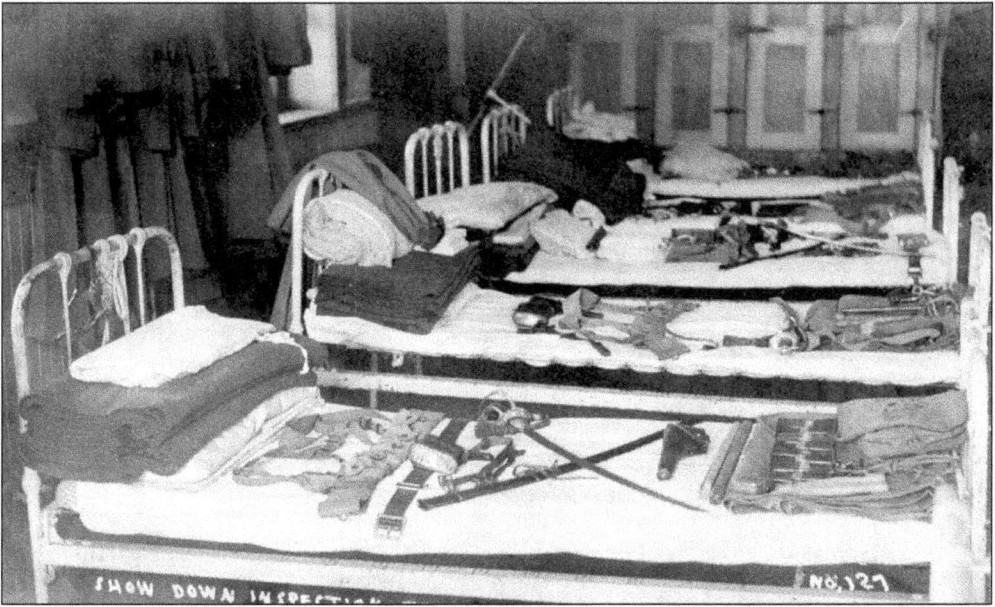

BARRACKS INSPECTION. Pictured here is a soldier's kit prepared and ready for an officer's inspection. Periodic inspections by an officer ensured that a soldier and his equipment were ready for action immediately. This photograph of an early 20th century cavalrymen's barracks shows all the accoutrements that a soldier needs for campaigning in the field. On the bunk are a trooper's saber, pistol, cartridge belt, haversack, blankets, canteen, and linen. Hanging on the bedstead are the soldier's spurs, the mark of a cavalryman.

CLEANING MESS EQUIPMENT. Maintaining equipment was—and will always be—an important responsibility in the Army. Several members of the Thirteenth Cavalry are cleaning mess equipment on the barracks porch while another trooper's wash is left on the line to dry.

INTERIOR OF QUARTERS

ENLISTED QUARTERS INTERIOR. This picture shows the interior of the cavalry enlisted men's barracks at the end of the 19th century. At the foot of the soldier's cots are footlockers where men stored their clothing and accoutrements. In the center of the room is a rifle stand where the rifles were stored. Notice several locks on the stand that secured the weapons. Apparently, the troops are out on duty as only one M1896 Krag-Jorgensen carbine remains in the rack.

SOLDIERS' DIET. Soldiers were always looking for ways to add variety to their diet. A soldier's diet in the 19th century American Army was as dull as the daily routine of military life. Typical rations of the period consisted of beans, hardtack, salt bacon, coffee, flour, range beef, and coarse bread. Here, a group of soldiers have returned from a hunt that netted numerous wild turkeys that flourished on the Kansas plains.

MOUNTED DRESS PARADES. Dress parades were important moments in the weekly routine of a cavalry troop. Spit and polish were put to the test. This snapshot in time captures a group of soldiers from the Third United States Cavalry in 1892 preparing for such an inspection.

SNAKE MAN. Soldiers of the Second Cavalry Regiment are pictured here while taking a break from their duties in the field. In 1900, United States Army soldiers were still clad in dark blue wool shirts and light blue kersey trousers. All of the soldiers in this picture wear the standard issue brownish-colored, wide-brimmed hats. It was not until the end of the first decade of the 20th century that American soldiers were issued warm weather khaki uniforms. Note the soldier in the center of the picture with a rattlesnake draped around his neck.

NINTH CAVALRY. Buffalo soldiers pose outside of their barracks located around the Cavalry Parade Field. In the early years of the 20th century, an African-American cavalry regiment, the Ninth, was posted to Fort Riley. Most of the soldiers in this photograph wear the uniform prescribed by the 1902 General Uniform Regulations that signaled a significant departure from the cavalry uniforms of the late 19th century. Gone were the dark blue Prussian style uniforms with plumed helmets, as a simpler and more functional uniform was adopted. Notice the man with his back to the camera, third from the right, who is wearing an 1880 pattern white summer helmet. These issue helmets were made of cork and covered with a bleached or unbleached cotton drilling.

COOKS AND BAKERS. A Cooks and Bakers School was established in the first decade of the 20th century to instruct soldiers in food preparation. Cooks and bakers were also instructed in the proper methods of preparing food in the field. Bakers learned to construct field ovens in order to bake bread in the field.

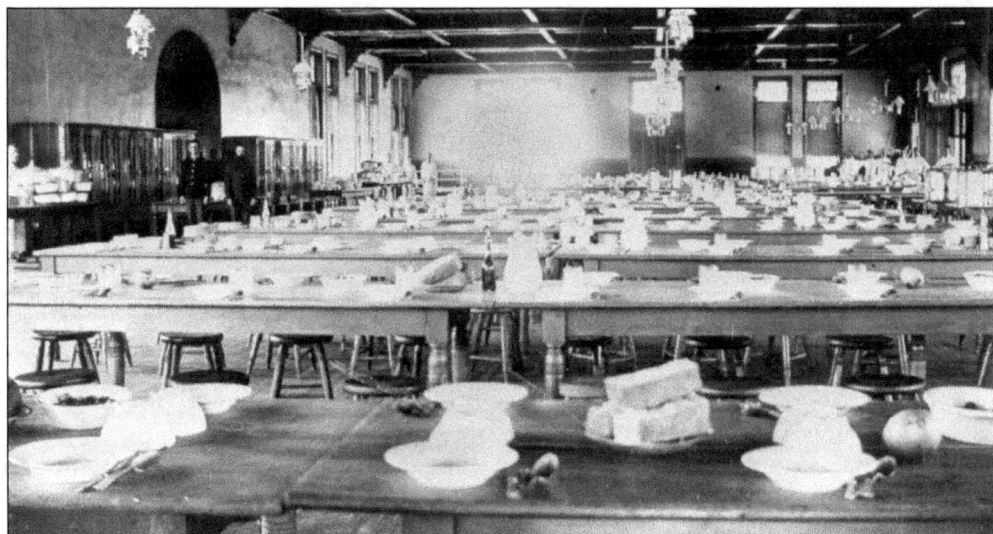

MESS HALL. By the early 20th century, consolidated mess halls had replaced the company mess of the "old Army." Soldiers no longer prepared their own meals but relied on enlisted men who were specifically trained in food preparation and were assigned to cook meals for their comrades. Building 210 served as a common mess hall for the entire post. Here, soldiers received three meals a day. A cavalry trooper's typical meal in 1908 included a substantial breakfast of steamed rice with sugar and cream, stewed prunes, Irish stew, toast, bread, and coffee; a hearty lunch of cream of tomato soup, roast ribs of beef, mashed potatoes, lima beans, steam pudding, lemon sauce, onions, pickles, and bread; and a light supper of chili stew, baked potatoes, apple sauce, hot rolls, and tea.

MAKING DONUTS. Cooks and bakers learn to make donuts, as shown in this June 1909 photo. Private Sissenwine (fourth from the right) holds a finished product. The United States Army established the Training School for Bakers and Cooks at Fort Riley in February 1905. Initially, the school received little attention from the post commanders, as many of the students sent there were considered troublemakers and problem soldiers. In March 1906, Post Commander Colonel Godfrey ordered the school be cleaned up. It was largely due to the efforts of Captain L.R. Holbrook and Color Sergeant Patrick Dunne that the institution became a model program.

BARRACKS RECREATION. In the early 20th century, the United States Army attempted to improve the quality of life for the average soldier. Providing the soldiers with amenities kept morale up during long periods of inactivity and cut down on the likelihood of trouble. In this picture, soldiers were supplied with a pool table in their barracks, which offered recreation in their off-duty hours.

CAVALRYMEN TRAINING WITH THEIR HORSES. Pictured are the cavalrymen of Troop "B", Sixth Regiment of Cavalry training at Fort Riley in 1896. The troopers are using their horses for cover while practicing defensive methods for repulsing an attack. They are wearing the late 19th century uniform that consisted of khaki riding pants with a dark blue, wool service blouse. Each soldier is using a M1896 Krag-Jorgensen carbine. This weapon, of Norwegian design, replaced the single-shot Springfield and was the first magazine feed weapon adopted by the United States Army.

FIELD ARTILLERY BATTERY. A field artillery battery ready for action on the Fort Riley Artillery Parade Field in the late 19th century. A four-gun artillery battery is unlimbered with crews standing ready. Behind the guns are the limbers that haul the cannons into action. Limbers not only pulled the guns into action, but carried a chest with a small amount of ammunition. To the rear of the limbers are the caissons, identified by the spare wheel, that supply additional ammunition for each of the cannons. The building the battery faces, in the center of the photograph, is the headquarters building for the Field Artillery School.

PISTOL INSPECTION. In this photograph, a sergeant is inspecting the pistols of a squad outside an enlisted men's barracks. All of these soldiers are carrying a .45 caliber Colt New Service revolver. This particular side arm was the last revolver issued by the United States Army. Within two years, this weapon was replaced by the Colt Model 1911 .45 caliber automatic pistol. Notice the soldier in the forage cap and the white duck fatigue jacket leaning over the porch observing the proceedings.

RIFLE AND CARBINE TARGET PRACTICE. Rifle and carbine target shooting were important in maintaining military proficiency. Training in marksmanship became especially important after such engagements as the Rosebud and Little Bighorn in 1876. Apparently, one group of soldiers decided to spend an afternoon honing their skills at the barracks, rather than in the field. Note the target on the left side of the barracks, near the stairs.

MOUNTED SERVICE SCHOOL. The Mounted Service School, established in September 1907, included both the cavalry and the field artillery arms of the service. According to Brigadier General Edward S. Godfrey, the mission of the new school was to instruct candidates in the combined operations of the cavalry and the artillery. The crest of the school, designed by Colonel George H. Cameron, reflected the dual disciplines of the institution. The shield was divided into two portions, the top half was in yellow for the cavalry and the lower half represented the artillery, in red. The winged spur symbolized the Department of Equitation and the winged horseshoe signified the Department of Hippology. The school remained in service at Fort Riley until 1919 when the cavalry and artillery components were separated by the War Department.

CAVALRY SCHOOL. Knowing how to keep the horse healthy and ready for field use was an important part of a cavalryman's training. Pictured here is a group of Cavalry School students examining the horse's foot to determine the animal's soundness.

FUNERAL OF PRIVATE DANIEL. Military funerals are often occasions of pomp and pageantry. Soldiers pay their final respects to a fallen comrade with music, salutes, eulogies, and unit traditions. In this picture the men of Battery A, Sixth Field Artillery say goodbye to Private Daniel, a member of their unit, on a fall day in October 1909. Fort Riley's military cemetery is located northwest of the main post, near the Republican River.

FUNERAL PROCESSION OF PRIVATE DANIEL. This picture shows the funeral procession of Private Daniels as it makes its way to the cemetery just beyond the main post. Leading the procession was the Sixth Artillery's band and the caisson bearing the body of the fallen soldier, behind follows the mourners, which include Daniel's fellow soldiers. In the background, the buildings surrounding both the Cavalry Parade Field and the Artillery Parade are seen in the distance.

POLO. An important activity at the Fort Riley Cavalry School was polo. The commander and the teaching staff of the school actively encouraged the game. While it was considered a recreational pastime, the sport did sharpen the student's equestrian skills and was therefore considered beneficial to cavalrymen. There was no shortage of prospective players and Fort Riley was able to field a significant number of teams. As such, teams at Fort Riley were placed in one of three groups: the Academic Division group, the Second Cavalry group, and the Separate Units group. For example, in 1927, the Academic Division fielded five teams: the Second Division four teams, and the Separate Units put two teams into competition. The teams not only played each other, but also participated in games that involved teams located at other cavalry posts. In 1913, Fort Riley's Mounted Service School team won the All Army Championship. The photograph shows the members of 1913's winning team.

CHILDREN WITH PONIES. These two children pose with their ponies outside the officers' quarters on Forysth Avenue. Within the cavalry, a horse culture existed and all dependents were encouraged to ride. On weekends, whole families would take part in horse-related activities like fox hunting, polo, or riding for pleasure.

REPUBLICAN RIVER BRIDGE AFTER THE FLOOD JUNE 22. 1915. JUNCTION CITY KANS

FLOODS. There have been significant floods along the Republican River throughout the 20th century. Noteworthy floods occurred in 1915, 1935, and 1951. In June 1915, floodwaters destroyed the Republican River Bridge that connected Junction City, Kansas with Fort Riley.

Three

THE GREAT WAR
AND CAMP FUNSTON
1917–1919

RECRUITS. Volunteers are welcomed to Camp Funston with a band leading them into their new surroundings. With the massive influx of volunteers, construction crews at the fort struggled to build quarters to accommodate the new citizen soldiers. The buildings in the background are in various stages of construction. This group is just arriving with suitcases and bags in hand to begin a 12 to 16 week course of basic training.

NEW ARRIVALS. New recruits arrive at Camp Funston, Fort Riley, Kansas c. 1917. With the United States' entry into World War I in April of 1917, the army's ability to absorb the new soldiers was stretched to the limit. Over 4,000,000 civilians were inducted into the army, and arming, equipping, and training these soldiers required a monumental effort. Upon arrival at Fort Riley, these recruits would shed their civilian clothes and receive their khaki uniforms. It would take these new citizen soldiers some time to pack their newly acquired gear in correct military fashion. Eventually, nearly 50,000 men trained at Funston during World War I.

CAMP FUNSTON. America was woefully unprepared when it entered World War I in April 1917. Cantonments and training camps to handle the massive influx of soldiers created by the draft sprang up all over the country. Just after America's entry into the war, Fort Riley was designated as a divisional training post. Camp Funston, five miles east of the main post, became an overnight creation of semi-permanent wooden buildings and tents. America's lack of preparedness was most evident in the first draftees who arrived at camp. These men wore overalls and trained with wooden guns because their uniforms and weapons had not yet been produced. This picture depicts the temporary nature of the camp as tents serve as barracks for the large number of trainees due to arrive. Eventually, over 1,400 structures would be built at this camp.

GENERAL LEONARD WOOD. General Leonard Wood took command of Camp Funston in 1917 and oversaw the training of the Tenth and Eighty-ninth Divisions during World War I. Pictured outside of his hilltop headquarters, General Wood (second from the left) poses with his staff. Today, only the stone foundation and the chimney remain.

Gen. View, Camp Funston, Kans.

VIEWS OF FUNSTON. Two views of Camp Funston from General Leonard Wood's headquarters. Wood's headquarters were located on a high hill that overlooked the massive army camp, which was hastily built just after America entered World War I. Looking down the from the hill, Wood could survey the nearly 1,400 wooden structures that made up this 2,000-acre training facility.

30 A General View of Camp Funston, Ka.

Kansas Bldg. Camp Funston Kans.

KANSAS AND NEBRASKA BUILDING. The soldiers who came to Camp Funston during World War I were drawn mostly from the states surrounding Kansas. Kansas and Nebraska erected buildings to accommodate the men from their states and give them a few of the comforts of home. Pictured here are the Kansas (*above*) and Nebraska (*below*) buildings.

Neb. Bldg. Camp Funston, Ka

RECRUITING VEHICLE. Despite men rushing to enlist in the Army after war was declared in April 1917, recruiting officers would travel from the fort to solicit additional volunteers. This vehicle was used to travel into surrounding communities to sign men up for military service.

WORLD WAR I BLACK SOLDIERS. Two World War I black soldiers pose outside their barracks at Camp Pawnee, Fort Riley, Kansas. Camp Pawnee was the African-American camp located two miles west of Camp Funston. More than 350,000 African Americans served in the armed forces during World War I. While many of these troops were eager to fight, the majority of them were assigned to segregated support units. Some all-black units, like the 365th Infantry Regiment of the 92nd Infantry Division did, however, see action in France.

WORLD WAR I FULL KIT A picture of a World War I soldier in full kit outside of his barracks, 1917 to 1918. This particular soldier, ready to leave for the front in France, wears an olive drab overseas cap, an M1910 cartridge belt with five pocket sections, an M1910 canteen that held one quart of liquid, and a long pack. The soldier is armed with a 1917 rifle and bayonet.

MILITARY POLICE. Ever since the 17th century, military police duties were delegated to a small body of select troops. These duties included keeping order among the troops, enforcing military regulations, controlling traffic, investigating crimes on post, and protecting government property. This picture shows a military policeman from the World War I era, along with his vehicle at Camp Funston. It is unknown if the dog was assigned to the military police, was a unit mascot, or if the animal had just wandered into the picture.

WORLD WAR I FOXHOLE. A World War I recruit undergoes trench warfare training at Fort Riley, preparing to go "over there." The American soldiers, known as "doughboys," were instructed in an environment that simulated the conditions of the western front. This soldier appears to be armed with a Lebel rifle and is wearing a helmet based on a British design. On his chest, the soldier has a box-type respirator gas mask, also of British design, which can be seen above his right forearm.

WORLD WAR I MEAL. World War I era soldiers preparing a meal in the field, *c.* 1918. Providing combat troops with regular hot meals was an important factor in maintaining an army's morale. The distribution of meals to frontline troops, however, was extremely difficult. Authorities recognized the need for hot, high-quality food to be distributed by field kitchens as close to the front as possible and developed containers and cooking utensils to easily transport the food rations.

DIPPING HORSES. In the days before commercial insecticide sprays for horses, cavalrymen protected their mounts from pests by dipping them in a home brewed concoction. These World War I era soldiers are preparing to send a horse through a long trough filled with the fly repellent. Note the long lead line intended to guide the horse through to the other side.

PONTOON BRIDGE. Throughout history, rivers have often presented major obstacles for military troops on the move. When bridges are absent, field commanders must find other means for moving soldiers and equipment across rivers. Military engineers have long considered the problem and their solution has been the pontoon bridge. Pontoon bridges have existed since ancient times, when the Greek historian Herodotus described the Persian Army's bridge across the Hellespont. Modern army engineers carry specialized equipment, including pontoons and bridging material that is assembled quickly to span a river. This photograph depicts a World War I era artillery unit crossing the Republican River near Junction City, Kansas.

MOUNTED MACHINE GUN UNIT. This photo depicts a 1920s machine gun unit, photographed on the Artillery Parade Field. The unit, lead by a Sergeant Fourth Grade, consisted of mounted machine gunners and their equipment. Both the .30 caliber machine gun and its ammunition are packed on the Phillips cavalry packsaddle. The designer of the Phillips, Major Albert E. Phillips, Tenth Cavalry, learned the difficulties of packing heavy equipment on horses. In the early 1920s, cavalry units received Phillips packsaddles for the .30 caliber, water-cooled machine gun. The machine gun is mounted on the center horse, while the ammunition is packed on the horses at the left.

Zonc . Camp Funstan . Kans

ARMY CITY. Army City, Camp Funston, *c.* 1918. Called the "zone" by the soldiers at Camp Funston, Army City was a commercial area located just east of the army camp alongside the Kansas River on the Pawnee Flats. The city was about four city blocks in length and it was built expressly for the purposes of entertaining the soldiers. The area consisted of hotels, clothing stores, a movie theater, pool hall, and an arcade. Army city ceased to exist in the early 1920s when many of the businesses were destroyed by a fire.

AERO SQUADRON AT "THE ZONE" CAMP FUNSTON, KAS. 5-18-19

ARMY CITY AND BIPLANES. Another view of Army City, May 5, 1918. In the foreground are a line of Curtiss JN-4 "Jenny" biplanes of the Army Air Corps. The Jenny never saw action in World War I, but was responsible for training thousands of American airmen for service in France. These biplanes, a popular added attraction, flew in from Love Field, to promote enlistments in the Army.

57

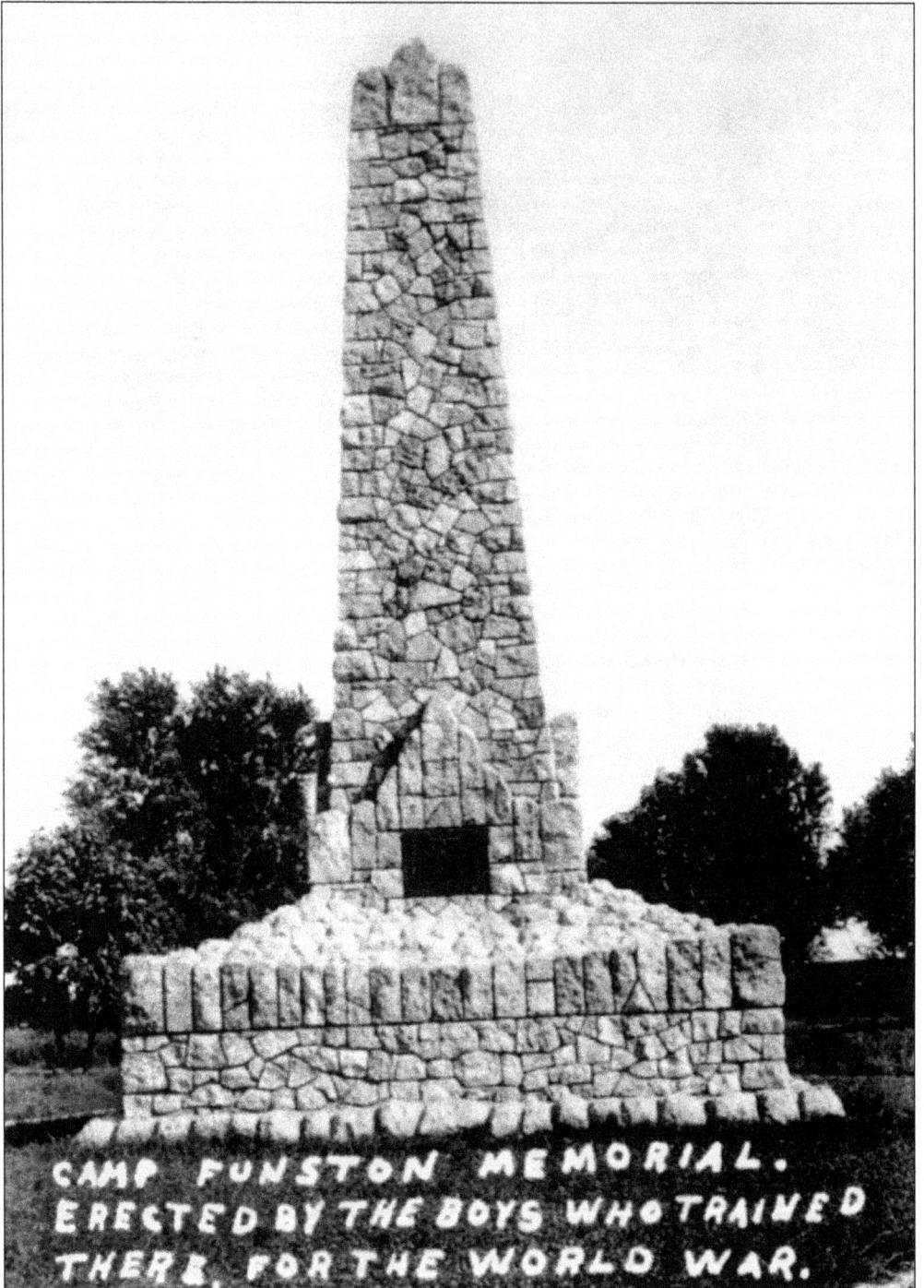

WORLD WAR MEMORIAL. By order of General Leonard Wood, the Commander of Camp Funston during World War I, a stone obelisk was constructed after the war to commemorate the memory of those soldiers who trained at Camp Funston in 1917 and 1918. The monument was dedicated in September 1919.

Four

FORT RILEY DURING THE INTERWAR YEARS: 1919–1941

CAVALRY SCHOOL. The Cavalry School established at Fort Riley in 1919 replaced the Mounted Service School. After World War I, the Mounted Service School was reorganized for cavalry only, as the field artillery was now given its own separate school. Colonel George H. Cameron once again designed the crest of the new cavalry institution. Cameron's design reflected the principle disciplines taught at the school. The shield's field was yellow, the color of the United States Cavalry; the saber represented the Department of Weapons; the winged spur symbolized the Department of Equitation; and the book and lamp denoted academic subjects. The Latin motto under the shield, *Mobilitate Vigemus*, means Mobility and Vigilance when translated.

FIELD ARTILLERY ON CUSTER HILL. A field artillery battery charges up Custer Hill during maneuvers in the 1920s. By the beginning of the 20th century all artillerymen rode into battle with the battery. Each gunner had both an assigned duty when firing the gun, and a specific place when riding into action. One artilleryman rode on the left side of the first pair of horses, the lead pair, the second man rode with the next pair, the swing pair, and a third rode the with the horses closest to the limber, the wheel pair. Four other artillerymen were seated on either the limber or with the cannon. Two of these two men rode on top of the ammunition chest on the limber and the other two men rode on seats placed on either side of the cannon barrel. Moreover, the harness of the gun team was specifically designed to facilitate the quick removal and replacement of either injured or dead horses.

THIRTEENTH CAVALRY CROSSING THE REPUBLICAN. The Thirteenth Cavalry Regiment was assigned to the Cavalry School during the 1930s as part of the school cadre. Pictured here are troopers from that Regiment fording the Republican River in the spring of 1933.

SABER DRILL - FORT RILEY.

SABER DRILL. The saber drill was an extremely difficult technique to master. A cavalryman was required to control a galloping horse while wielding a saber. The 1913 Model Cavalry Saber carried by the cavalrymen was a straight-bladed, two-edged weapon that was intended for both stabbing and slashing. Lieutenant George Patton purportedly designed this sword in 1912 and 1913, the last pattern of sword adopted by the United States Cavalry. In this photograph the drill was made even more complicated, as the horse was required to jump an obstacle just before the trooper struck at the target.

HORSE-MOUNTED RADIO. In the 1930s, modern field communication equipment was adapted to horse mounted cavalry units. Radio receiver (SCR 163A), antenna, and generator, all 206 pounds, mounted on a Phillips packsaddle. The photograph shows the headquarters radiomen in action sending and receiving messages. Note the hand crank generator that supplied power to the radio located at the base of the antenna.

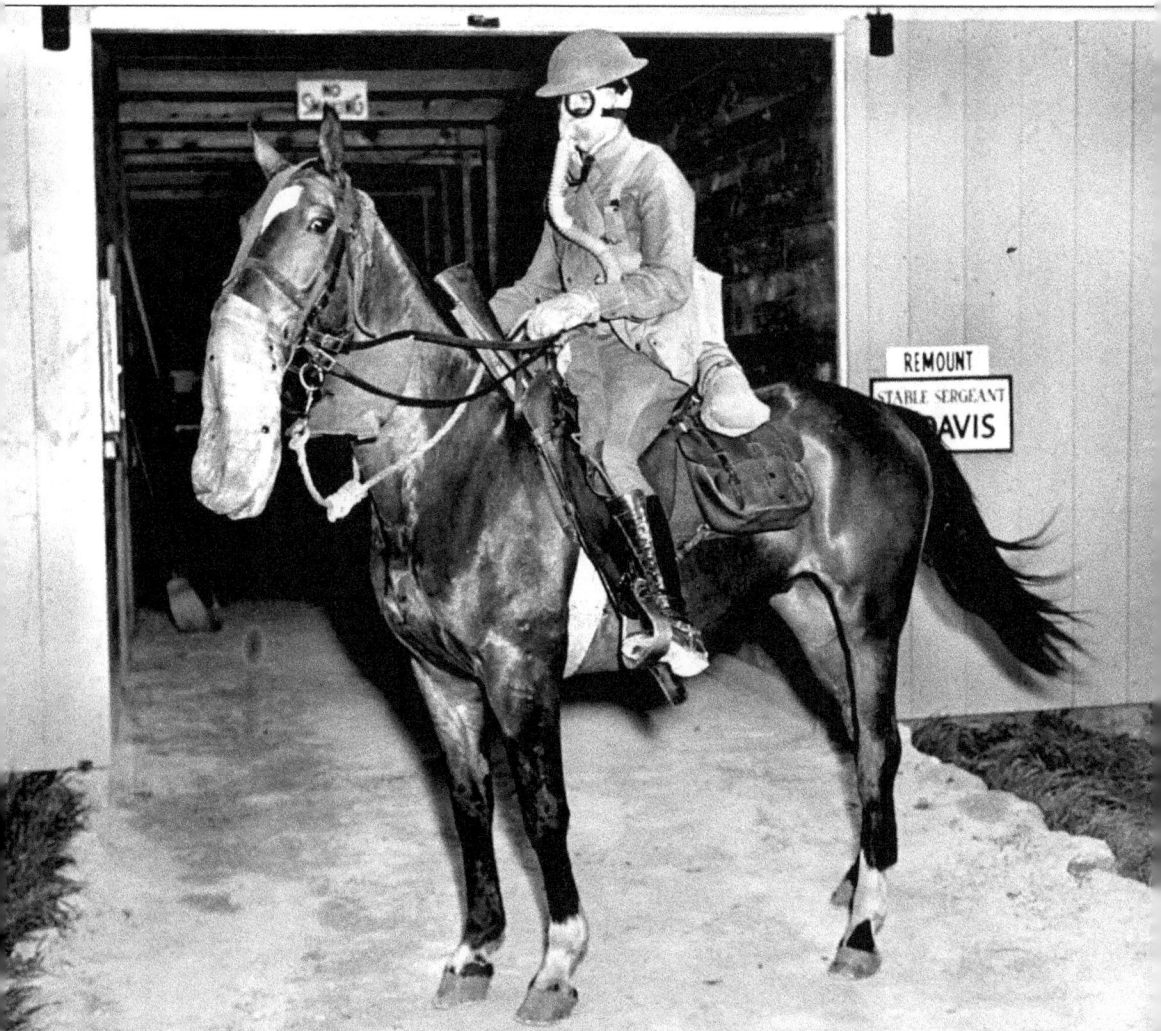

GAS MASK. A cavalryman equipped for chemical warfare, Fort Riley, 1941. World War I combat introduced poison gas attacks. During the interwar period, the United States Army believed that gas would be used again, and prepared for chemical warfare. The horse in this picture, however, was unprotected and wears an Army issue feedbag. The United States developed equine respirators during World War I, but only issued them to the cavalry units in limited quantities.

MONKEY DRILL. It was typical for the cavalrymen to spend considerable time in the saddle. The primary concern of a new recruit was to learn to simply stay on his mount. Officers and non-commissioned officers worked tirelessly to turn their men into competent and confident riders. Soldiers who mastered the techniques of riding began to look for a means that displayed their ability. One such method was performing the "monkey drill," which was a variation on Roman riding. Veteran troopers and their horses would often perform astounding feats of riding and jumping. Shown here are a few samples of amazing feats of horsemanship by Fort Riley troopers.

HORSE JUMPING THROUGH HUMAN PYRAMID. A cavalry trooper and his horse jump over a table and through a human pyramid on the Cavalry Parade Field.

HORSE JUMPING TABLE. Here a cavalryman and horse clear a table occupied by two fellow troopers.

CEMETERY HILL. Cavalrymen were continuously testing their riding skills and abilities. One such exercise, called the "Russian Ride," consisted of a weekend three-mile ride. The ride comprised twenty-four jumps of varying degrees of difficulty. While jumping over unusual obstacles rarely occurred in real-world situations, the ride was instrumental in instilling confidence in a rider's ability. Moreover, before a student could graduate from the Cavalry School the trooper was expected to successfully negotiate the dreaded "Cemetery Hill." As the picture shows, the hill would test both the trooper's riding agility and his courage.

STEEPLECHASE. Spectators watching the action at a United States Army-sponsored steeplechase competition in the late 1930s. Throughout the first three decades of the 20th century, the army actively promoted mounted sports at the fort. The polo fields, at Republican Flats, were used for both horse races and steeplechases. Beside steeplechases, the cavalrymen participated in horse racing, polo, and endurance riding. One of the most notable races at Fort Riley took place in 1904 between an automobile and a horse. Louis Loeb, the owner of a new Cadillac, matched his vehicle against Dr. Fred O'Donnell's fine thoroughbred hunter. The race, witnessed by a considerable crowd, saw O'Donnell's horse easily beat Loeb's horseless carriage.

THE *Rasp.* The *Rasp*, the student yearbook of the Cavalry School, captured the routine and challenges of being a student at the Mounted Service School. The yearbook was published each year and contained a variety of articles. The 1914 edition of the *Rasp* considered such topics as "The Types of Saddle Horses," "Breeds of Horses," "Mounted Swordsmanship," and "Polo in the Army." The annual also poked fun at the assorted students who took part in the course. Pictured above is one such cartoon that depicted the trials and tribulations endured by Mounted Service School students.

GROOMING. Cavalry enlisted men check the feet of their horses outside the unit's stables in 1941. Each troop of cavalry required two stables to house their horses. Each wooden stable measured 158 feet by 46 feet and quartered 58 horses. The care, feeding, and watering of horses were the responsibility of the troopers. Moreover, many cavalry officers recognized that only constant practice could turn these new equestrians into confident and accomplished riders.

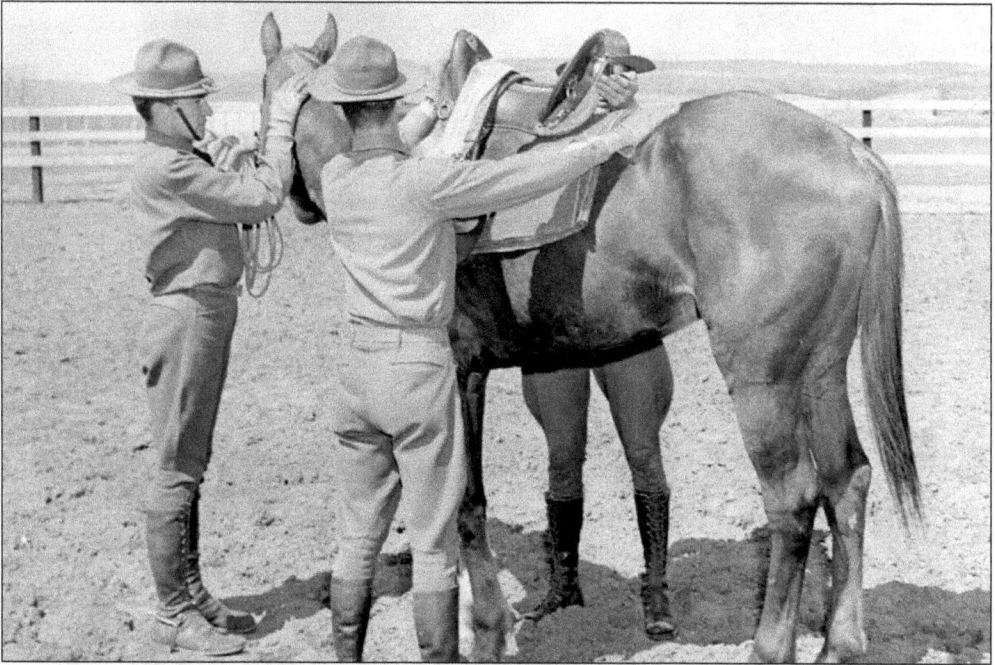

SADDLING AND BRIDLING. Cavalry instructors teach new recruits the proper methods in the saddling and bridling of a horse at the Fort Riley Cavalry School in 1941. Here a recruit saddles his horse under the watchful eyes of his instructor. Union General George B. McClellan developed this saddle shortly before the American Civil War. The McClellan Saddle went through many modifications, but remained the standard issue saddle for American cavalry troopers for almost 100 years.

BLACKSMITH AND FARRIERS. Blacksmiths and farriers kept the cavalry moving in the field. Field forages and other equipment were vital to this aspect of cavalry readiness. These enlisted specialties were the "mechanics" that kept the cavalry moving.

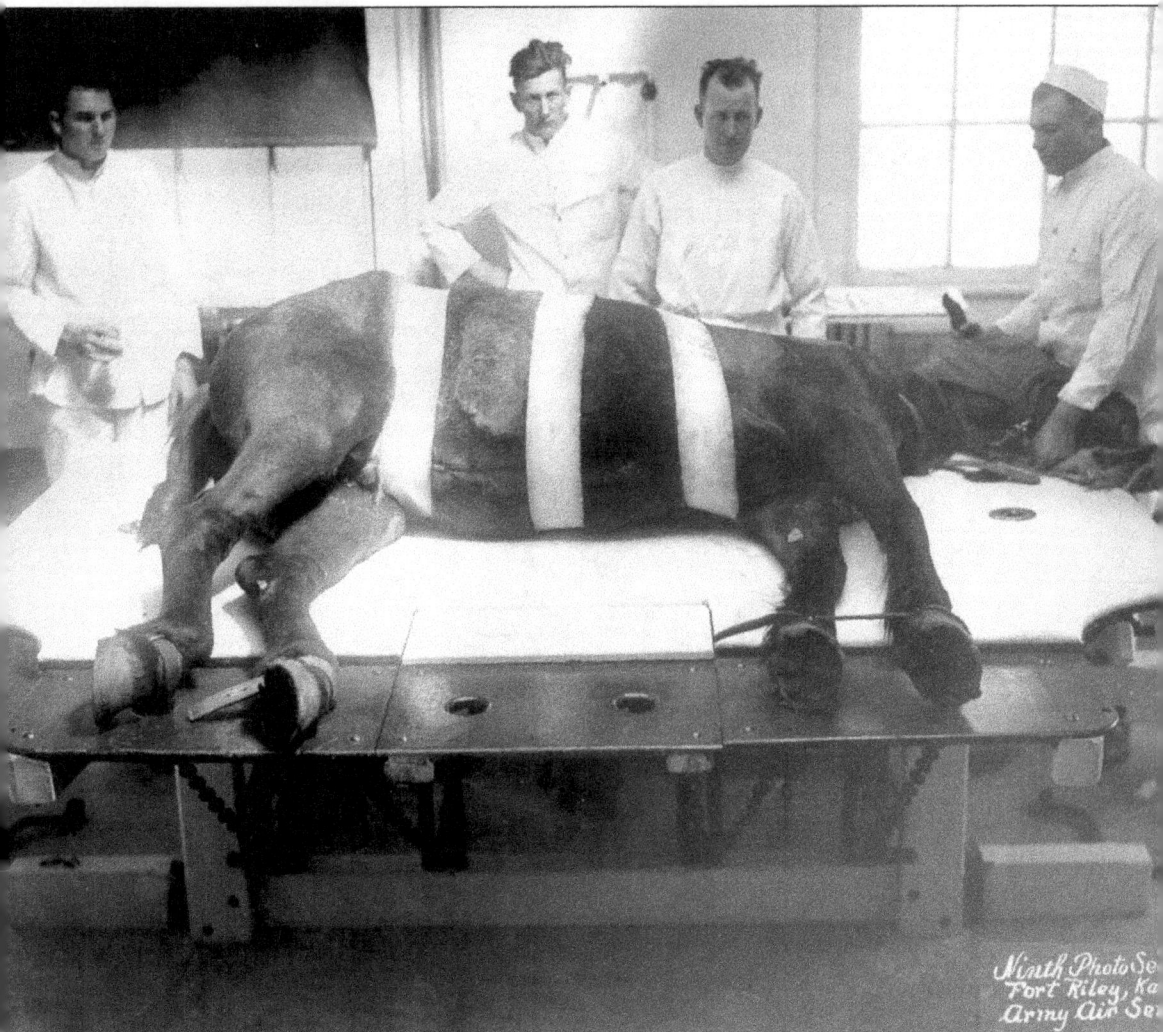

Ninth Photo Se
Fort Riley, Ka
Army Air Se

VETERINARIANS. The care and treatment of horses was vital to maintaining the readiness of cavalry units. Veterinarians were critical in ensuring the health and well being of the troopers' mounts. Occasionally, Army veterinarians were called upon to perform medical procedures on special operating tables. In the photograph, an upright horse has been secured to a specially designed tilt table. The sedated animal was then rotated into position and the operation commenced.

CLASS OF ADVANCED EQUITATION. Fort Riley's 1938 Class of Advanced Equitation poses with post mascot "Henry." Candidates for the Advanced Equitation Class were selected from the outstanding graduates of the Troop Officers' Class. This class received little academic instruction but concentrated solely on the practical applications of equitation, horsemanship, and related equine subjects. Graduates of the class would then become instructors of equitation and horsemanship.

THE STANDARD

This paper is published without expense to the United States Government.

VOL. 2   FORT RILEY, KANSAS, NOVEMBER 9, 1923   NO. 5

(*above*) **MAP PRACTICE.** Every Friday afternoon, students of the Troop Officers Class would study map problems. The exercise consisted of solving tactical problems on topographical maps. Students' solutions to these problems would be graded and turned back to the class. In this photograph, the instructor is discussing the current problem on a 1:21,210 scale map of Fort Riley.

(*left*) *THE STANDARD.* In the 1920s, the Cavalry School published a weekly newspaper, *The Standard.* The paper mostly dealt with the current social happenings, events occurring on the post, local gossip, and military and horse related humor.

MOUNTED REVIEW. Reviews and parades were part of the glitter that was—and is—Army life. Pictured here is a mounted review on the Cavalry Parade field by the Second Cavalry in the early 1930s.

MAJOR GENERAL AND GERMAN OFFICER. United States Army Major General Herr, Commander of the Cavalry School and a Third Reich German cavalry officer enjoy a ride around Fort Riley in the late 1930s. During the interwar period a significant number of military officers from around the world inspected the Cavalry School at Fort Riley. Contacts with German cavalry officers were common after the United States Army's Equestrian team competed in the Berlin Olympics of 1936.

"THE HUNT." Activities related to horses brought the Fort Riley community together for social occasions. One of the popular weekend events that continued into the 20th century was the "hunt". These hunts were conducted complete with red hunting coats and hounds. Hunters and a pack of hounds would scour the woods and brush around the "Island" along the Republican River in search of quarry. There were few foxes, however, so hunters had to often content themselves with hunting jack rabbits and coyotes. Pictured here is a group of hunters and their dogs about to begin a "fox hunt."

FOX HUNTERS. Fox hunters in the woods near the Republican River. The dogs have begun to wade into the water while the hunters follow behind. Both men and women comprise the group who are out for the weekend entertainment. Notice the cluster of individuals in the center right of the picture—men in both military uniform and in the traditional hunt clothing are seen here.

OUR FIRST COYOTE HUNT—PACK OF PAWNEE HUNT CLUB.

PAWNEE HUNT CLUB IN THE RASP. The *Rasp*, the student yearbook of the Cavalry School, takes an amusing view at one of the highpoints of Fort Riley society; the hunt. The *Rasp* was a product of the student officers enrolled at the school. Issues of the annual often took a humorous and irreverent look at the activities of the Cavalry School. As such, these yearbooks offer a wealth of material concerning the lifestyles of the officer students.

PAWNEE HUNT CLUB. Hunters and hounds prepare for the hunt on the plains of Kansas. Notice the man holding a large horn preparing to announce the beginning of the hunt.

TUTTLE'S DINING ROOM. A dinner party in an officer's quarters at Fort Riley in the 1930s. Seated in the dining room of Major Hiram Tuttle's home at 24 B Forsyth Avenue, from left to right, are Tuttle, Gale Fletcher, Robert Borg, Lieutenant Secondare, and Gladys Tuttle. Cavalry officers during the inter-period entertained themselves on post by hosting dinner parties, conducting polo matches, engaging in fox hunts, and organizing dances.

TUTTLE'S MANTLE. The mantle in the dining room of Major Hiram Tuttle's quarters at Fort Riley. In 1935, Tuttle and his wife Gladys occupied a home located at 24 B Forsythe Avenue. On the mantle are silver trophies won by Tuttle for equestrian events. On the wall are photographs of Tuttle on his prize-winning horses, Vast and Si Murray. In 1936, Tuttle was part of the United States Olympic Equestrian Team at the Berlin Olympics.

FORSYTHE AVENUE FLOOD. A row of officers' quarters on Forsyth Avenue flooded by the Kansas River in 1935. Floodwater from the river approached the front porches of officers' quarters in the summer of 1935. Hiram Tuttle took this photograph in front of his quarters. After the disastrous flood of 1951, Defense Department officials decided that all future development of the post was to be carried out on Custer Hill, which rises above the flood plain.

TORNADO. Each year, between March and July, tornadoes are a real danger in the plains states. Twisters, however, are known to strike year round and can occur even in the wintertime. In the 1930s and 1940s, they often struck with little warning. In the spring of 1942, this brave photographer snapped a remarkable picture of a tornado about to descend on Camp Forsyth's building number 2100, the telephone and telegraph exchange.

SECOND CAVALRY CENTENNIAL. In 1936, the Second Cavalry Regiment observed its centennial. The Regiment put together a program that commemorated its frontier past. Participants dressed in period garb, danced, and celebrated the occasion with a cookout at Sturgis Field. In this photograph "cowboys" dance with their ladies while a string band plays.

LADIES' RIDING CLUB. The ladies' riding club, pictured outside of Wells Hall at Fort Riley in the late 1920s. Many of the wives of cavalry officers shared their husbands' interest in riding. Numerous riding, polo, and fox hunting clubs existed at Fort Riley in the first four decades of the 20th century. Often these clubs would unite in joint social functions with their civilian counterparts in nearby Junction City, Kansas. The Fort Riley Polo Club often played the Junction City team and it was noted that the rivalry promoted the vitality of the sport.

M 10,000. In the late 1930s, the M 10,000, Union Pacific's futuristic passenger train, visited Fort Riley. The train, the brainchild of Union Pacific's president Averell Harriman, was the prototype of a new generation of trains that, the railroad hoped, would eventually replace conventional steam locomotives. In February 1934, the revolutionary train began a tour of 22 states. One of its scheduled stops was Fort Riley. In this photograph, the M 10,000 approaches the post's main train station.

BOY SCOUT TROOP. Boy Scout Troop 117 consisted of African-American youngsters whose fathers were military personnel stationed at Fort Riley.

PORTEE. Porteeing of horses in the 1930s. In the 1930s the United States Army began to experiment with the motorization of the cavalry regiments. Traditional horse troopers believed that the horse-mounted soldiers could still perform vital military functions in difficult terrain. To save both the horse and rider the rigors of traveling to and from the battlefield, horses, and soldiers were trucked to the location, unloaded, and then sent to carry out their missions.

M2A2 Light Tank. In the summer of 1937, large-scale maneuvers involving horse and tank units were held at Fort Riley. This is a M2A2 Light Tank, assigned to the Thirty-fifth Tank Company, Thirty-fifth Infantry Division.

MOTORIZED SUPPORT VEHICLE. During the 1937 maneuvers, Cavalry units relied increasingly on motorized support vehicles for field operations. There was also the greater dependence on radio equipment to enhance battlefield communications. This radio vehicle was part of the Headquarters Company, Second Cavalry Regiment.

THIRTEENTH CAVALRY. During the interwar period, the United States Army began to experiment with the technological innovations that débuted during World War I. Among these advances were the additions of mechanization and aviation to the traditional branches of infantry, artillery, and cavalry. The transportation of horses in World War I vintage Liberty trucks was another experiment carried out in the late 1920s that married the traditional horse-mounted cavalry with the new motorized technology. Field exercises proved that hauling horses a portion of the distance could increase the range of the cavalry significantly. Like many interwar experiments, the porteeing of horses by the Thirteenth Cavalry was an ad hoc affair, as extra boards were bolted to the sides of the modified trucks. Moreover, there is no record of how the horses and soldiers faired riding on the solid rubber tires of these vehicles. At Fort Riley, Colonel Bruce Palmer, Assistant Commandant of the Cavalry School, and Colonel Charles L. Scott, Director of Instruction, made significant advances in the integration of mechanized vehicles with the horse-mounted cavalry.

MOTORCYCLE. A motorcycle troop of cavalrymen gather, preparing to move out in the early 1940s. These troopers have given up their horses for a new kind of mount—the motorcycle. Notice that these soldiers have retained the traditional cavalry uniform, including riding pants, boots, and spurs, but many of them have substituted helmets and goggles for their headgear. For easy access, these troopers have attached the rifle scabbards to the front wheel of their motorcycles.

COMMAND CAR. The command car of the First Cavalry Headquarters is pictured here, flanked by motorcycles at a review at "The Rimrock." The command-armored car offered the cavalry commander a mobile communications platform in which he could remain in radio contact with his troops in the field. By the late 1930s, motorization and mechanization were thoroughly integrated with the horse-mounted units of the United States Cavalry.

Army Planes, Fort Riley.

THOMAS MORSE. Above are two Thomas Morse 019 Scout observation aircrafts parked at Marshall Field, *c.* 1930s. In keeping with the Army's experimentation with new technology, the Chief of Cavalry Major General Herbert B. Crosby advocated, in 1928, that an observation squadron of the Air Corps be incorporated with the cavalry divisions to increase the unit's reconnaissance capabilities. These squadrons consisted of thirteen airplanes with a photographic section.

RIDERLESS HORSE. Military funerals have many traditions. One tradition that goes back to the time of Genghis Khan is the inclusion of a riderless horse in the funeral cortege. The riderless horse symbolizes that the fallen leader will no longer lead. This particular tradition has figured prominently in the funerals of military and political leaders such as George Washington, Abraham Lincoln, Douglas MacArthur, and John F. Kennedy. In the cavalry, troopers have also embraced the symbolism of the riderless horse. Other symbolic touches, like the soldier's boots thrust into the stirrups backwards and the cavalrymen's saber placed in a reverse position, emphasize the loss of a soldier. This picture, taken during the interwar period, shows the caparisoned riderless horse and his walker as they prepare to take part in a funeral at Fort Riley's cemetery.

Five

WORLD WAR II
FORT RILEY AND
THE GREAT CRUSADE

REVIEW OF TROOPS. A review of troops is an ancient ceremony dating back to Roman times. Along with the associated pageantry, a review also afforded the commander an opportunity to inspect the readiness of his command. This tradition and ceremony continues to the present day. In World War II, mounted reviews were conducted in the Camp Forsyth area of the Cavalry Replacement Training Center.

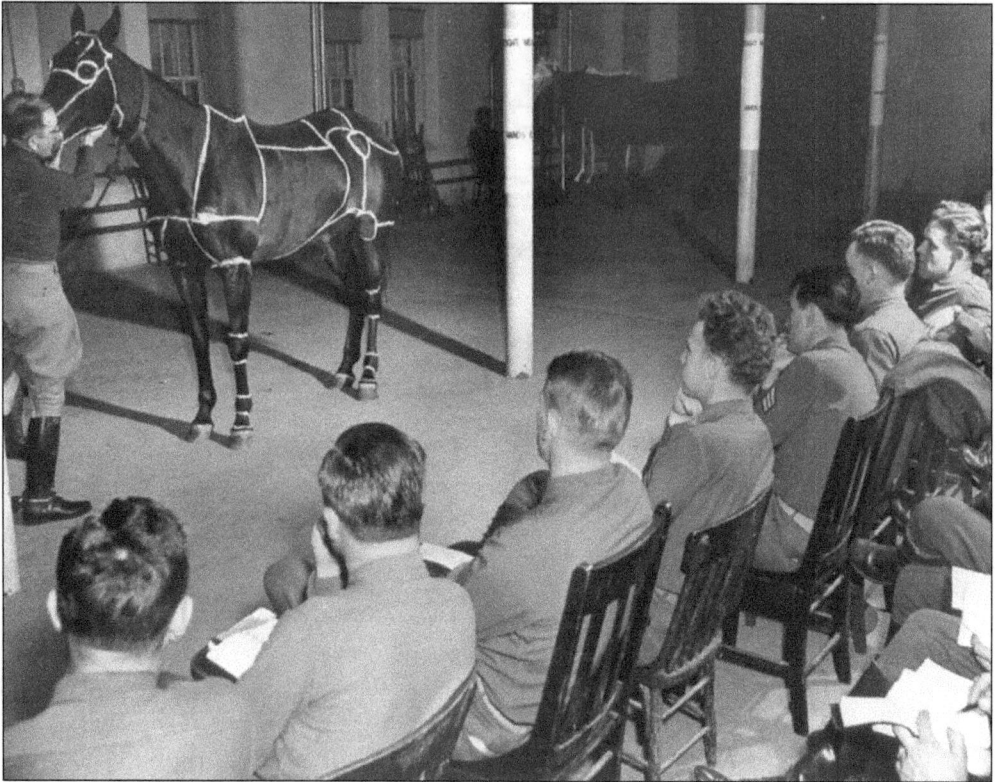

CAVALRY SCHOOL. Instruction in the Cavalry School included detailed coverage of the anatomy of the horse. Pictured here is a group of students during the early days of World War II, receiving instruction in this subject.

1941 EQUITATION CLASS. In equitation class a number of sergeants and corporals were instructed in the keeping of a proper seat while riding. In September 1919 the United States Army established the Cavalry School at Fort Riley. The school taught both officers and enlisted men the techniques and tactics of the cavalry. The courses taught to the students were equitation, horseshoeing, and the care and feeding of the horse.

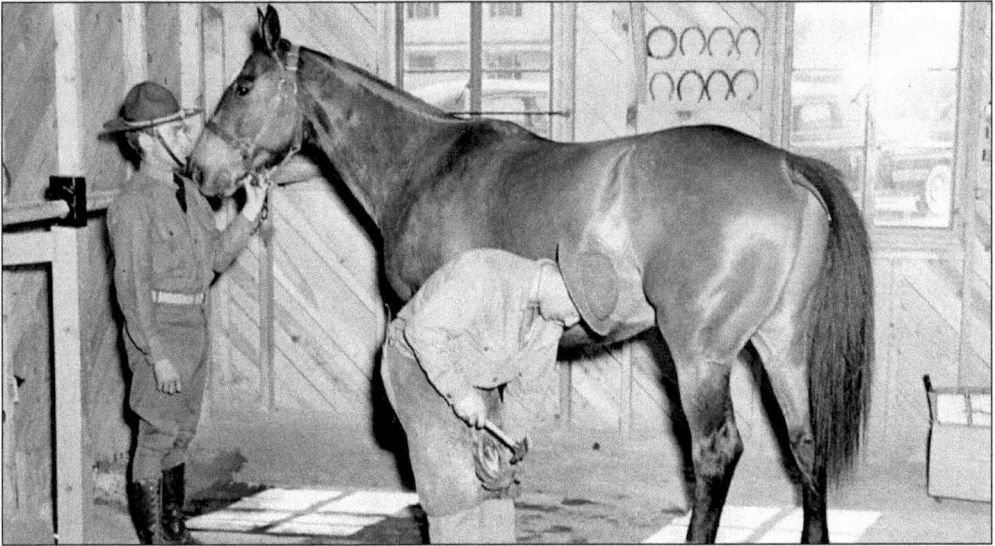

FARRIER. Pictured above is farrier shoeing a horse in the summer 1941. In December 1940, the Second Cavalry Division was assigned to Fort Riley. This division consisted of four cavalry regiments, the Second, Ninth, Tenth, and Fourteenth. Each regiment had a complement of farriers who looked after the shoeing of the regiment's horses. A horseshoeing school was set up within the Cavalry School in 1919 to train farriers for the United States Cavalry. The Cavalry School's Department of Horsemanship instructed students in the fundamentals of animal management, pack and wagon transportation, and horseshoeing. For many years, Frank Churchill, a civilian government employee, and teachers like him, taught the proper methods of shoeing a horse.

INSIDE OF BARRACKS 1941. Pictured are the barracks of Fort Riley's enlisted men. In the spring of 1941 Fort Riley annexed 32,370 acres, increasing the fort's size to nearly 53,000 acres. In addition to this expansion, the Army rebuilt Camp Funston to accommodate the increasing number of Americans who were inducted into the services. The barracks were Spartan by today's standards, but it gave the troops clean and comfortable housing while they trained at the post. Field equipment was placed on shelves; uniforms were hung below on a rack; and barracks bags, hats and towels were placed on nails. Nearly 125,000 men stayed in barracks like these at Fort Riley during World War II.

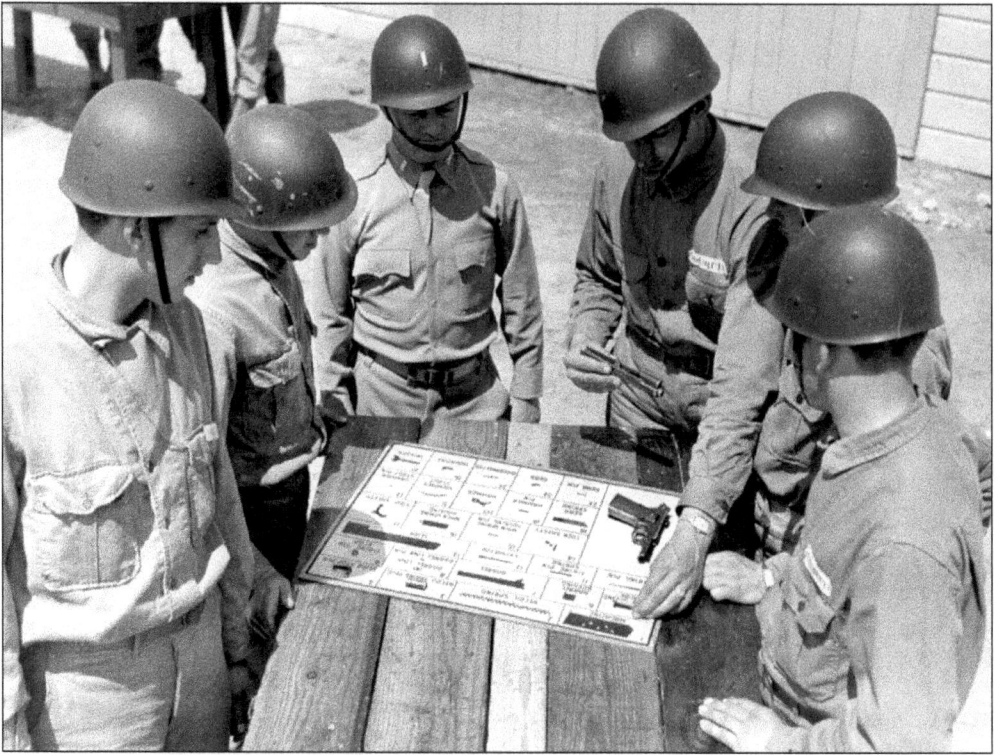

COLT .45 DISASSEMBLY. Cavalry troopers instructed in disassembling the Colt, Model 1911 .45 caliber automatic pistol. The ".45" was the standard sidearm of the cavalry from 1912 until the end of the horse-mounted cavalry in the 1950s. The chart on the table assisted the recruits in identifying the pistol's 27 component parts.

FIRING LINE IN SNOW. Winter on the Kansas plains can be bitterly cold and snowy. These soldiers, however, are not letting inclement weather disrupt their training schedule. Soldiers are firing M1 Garand rifles at targets at the base of the hill. The soldier sitting near the telephone is in communication with those soldiers who are operating the targets.

CLEANING RIFLE. The care and maintenance of his weapon is often critical to a combat soldier's well-being. Here a group of soldiers is learning to clean and assemble a 30 caliber M1 Garand semiautomatic rifle. The M1 was the soldier's standard weapon during World War II. More than 4,000,000 rifles were produced between 1941 and 1956. The rifle proved to be extremely reliable and it was not until 1957 that the M14 replaced it. In this picture, the rifle has been disassembled for cleaning.

CAVALRY RECRUIT TRAINING CENTER. The Cavalry Recruit Training Center trained soldiers in both mechanized and horse warfare. The United States Army intensified training after entering into World War II in December 1941. Courses for the troopers were 12 and 16 weeks in length, depending on the type of schooling assigned. Pictured here is a column of platoons, numbering approximately 800 men and horses.

95

POST MOVIE THEATER. Pictured is the Post Movie Theater at Camp Funston in 1941. Two enlisted men examine the movie posters placed outside of the theater. Movies, along with dances, polo, and horseback riding, provided recreation for the soldiers stationed at Fort Riley.

SNACK BAR. Snack bar servers at the Fort Riley's Camp Funston post canteen, 1941. The post canteen offered soldiers soups, fresh fruits, ice creams, and soft drinks. The post canteen also provided a social setting in which off-duty soldiers could relax and shoot the breeze with the table servers. During the wartime years, more then 125,000 troops passed through Fort Riley on their way overseas.

CATHOLIC MASS IN THE FIELD. During maneuvers in the field, chaplains who traveled with the troops conducted Sunday services. Chaplains of all denominations served in the United States Army. These men were commissioned officers and wore the appropriate uniform. During World War II, cartoonist Bill Mauldin commented that the average soldier had a lot of respect for the chaplains, as these dedicated men "kept up the spirits of the combat guys." In this picture from 1941, the Catholic priest is distributing communion to worshippers who have lined up in facing the stage.

LOUIS AND ROBINSON. During World War II, two legends in the world of sport trained at Fort Riley. These gentlemen were baseball great Jackie Robinson and boxing heavyweight champion, Joe Louis. In early 1942, Jackie Robinson, a semiprofessional basketball player from California was drafted into the Army and sent to Fort Riley, Kansas for basic training. After passing through basic training, Robinson applied to Officers Candidate School and passed all the requirements. Robinson, however, along with a number of other African-American officer candidates were rejected because of their race. At this time, heavyweight boxing champion Joe Louis was also posted to Fort Riley. Using his fame and popularity, Louis actively championed Robinson's cause. In time, Robinson and the other African-Americans were admitted to Officers Candidate School due largely to Louis' efforts. While at Fort Riley in 1942, these two champions posed together for a photograph.

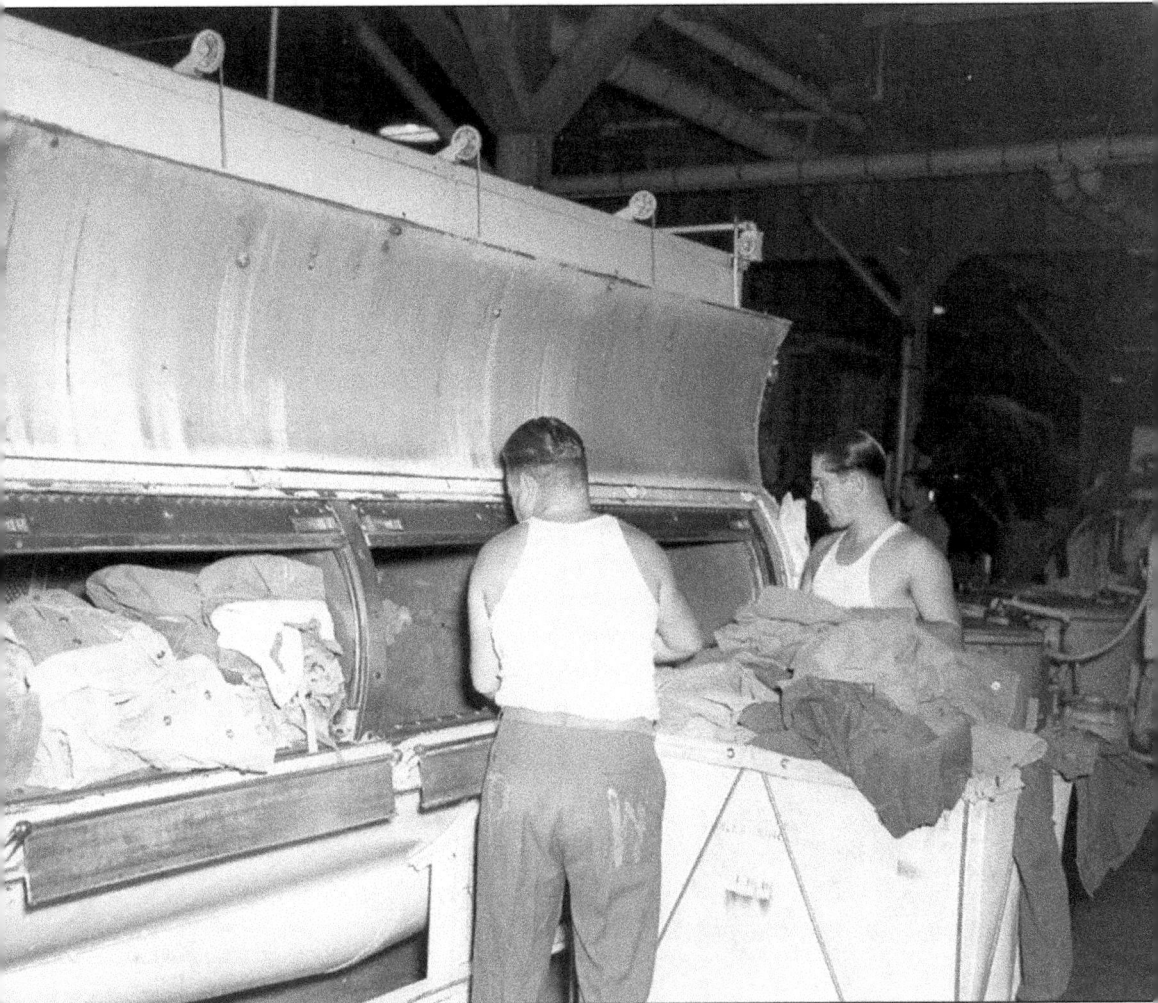

GERMAN POWS DOING LAUNDRY. After the defeat of the German Afrika Corps in the spring of 1943, thousands of German prisoners of war were sent to the United States. Fort Riley became one of thirteen camps selected to house the prisoners. One thousand POWs were housed in a portion of Camp Funston, located west of the main post. In this picture, two prisoners are loading laundry into a large washing machine. Note the large white letters "P W" on the seat of the prisoner's pants.

FRANKLIN D. ROOSEVELT TOUR. President Franklin D. Roosevelt visited Fort Riley while on a war inspection tour in the spring of 1943. The president's train arrived at the fort from Denver at 7:30, Easter morning. Shown here is the president riding with Kansas Governor Andrew F. Schoeppel.

FRANKLIN D. ROOSEVELT AT STURGIS FIELD. Easter Sunday took place at Sturgis Field on April 25, 1943. After initial briefings from the various unit commanders, a mounted cavalry unit escorted the president to Sturgis Field for Easter services.

FRANKLIN D. ROOSEVELT AT CEREMONY. Approximately 10,000 soldiers and 4,000 civilians attended the open-air ceremony. Upon conclusion of the services, Roosevelt received a tour of the fort including an inspection of the cavalry facilities and the Ninth Armored cantonment area. The president ended his stay by having lunch with 500 Cavalry officer candidates in the Cavalry Officers Mess.

143-504D-1-OBSN-GODND(12-27-40-504D)(2-500) CAV REPLACEMENT CENTER
FT RILEY KAN

CAVALRY REPLACEMENT TRAINING CENTER. Camp Forsyth, originally known as Republican Flats, was selected as the site for the Cavalry Replacement Training Center (CRTC). This aerial view shows the beginnings of this camp that began in 1940. Eventually, CRTC would train and deploy over 120,000 soldiers during World War II.

Six

Containment and Peacekeeping

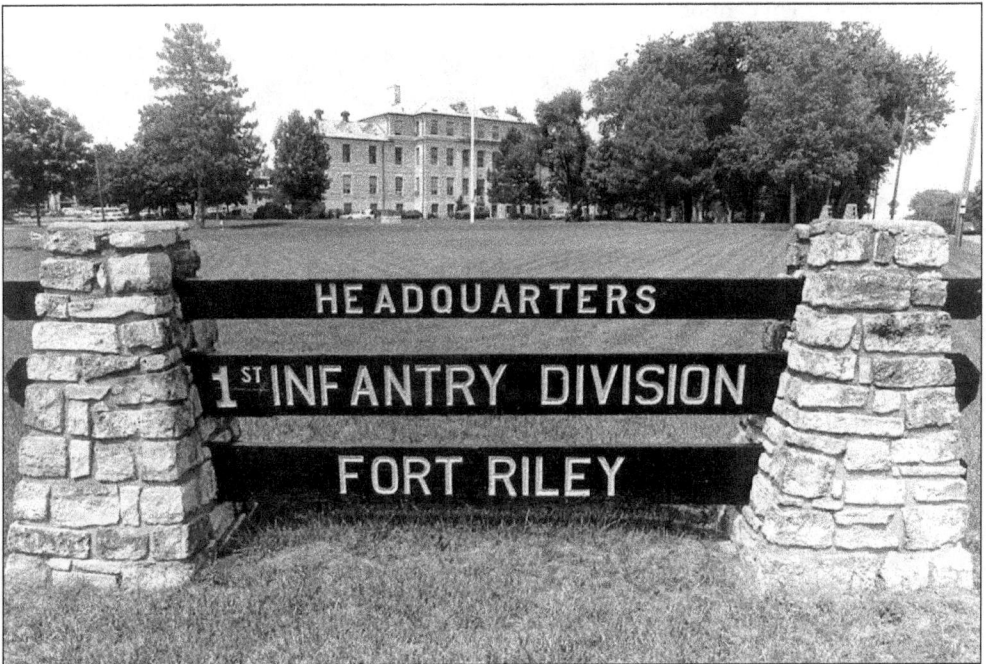

THE BIG RED ONE. In 1955, Fort Riley became the home of the First Infantry Division, called the Big Red One because of the soldiers' divisional shoulder patch that sported a large red numeral one. The division was headquartered in Summerall Hall, the post's former hospital building located on Huebner Avenue. During the Second World War, the First Infantry Division achieved an illustrious record campaigning in North Africa, Sicily, storming ashore on Omaha Beach, and repelling the German onslaught in the Ardennes.

M48 MEDIUM TANK. An M48 medium tank maneuvers across the plains of Kansas in the mid-1950s. Combat experience during the Korean War pointed out the deficiencies of the World War II M4 Sherman Tank. In the early 1950s, the Army began development on a successor to the Sherman. The result was the M48, designed by Chrysler and built by both the Ford Motor Company and General Motors. The tank carried a crew of four and was armed with a 90mm cannon.

GIS TRAINING IN FOXHOLE. The soldier furthest from the camera is firing an M60 general-purpose machine gun. The M60 machine gun replaced the World War II vintage .30 caliber Browning machine gun. The nearest soldier is firing an M-14 rifle, the standard issue weapon for infantrymen in the early 1960s. During the Cold War years, Fort Riley trained soldiers of the First Infantry Division who served in West Germany, Korea, and Vietnam.

104

MASTER SERGEANT CHARLES BROWN. Master Sergeant Charles Brown is pictured here in 1953 with Masquerader, a 1936 Olympic jumper. After the demobilization of the United States mounted forces in the early 1950s, the Army sent many of its retired show horses and cavalry horses to Fort Riley to live out the remainder of their lives.

HORSEPLAY. Two horses engage in some horseplay outside the stables at Fort Riley. During the mid-1950s, horses from the recently disbanded horse-mounted cavalry regiments were sent to Fort Riley to either be retired or sold to civilian buyers. The Army then turned the disposal process over to Department of Agriculture, which became the main agent for selling the livestock and cavalry equipment.

CHIEF. Chief was the last surviving United States Army Cavalry horse. The bay was foaled in 1932 and purchased for the Army in 1940, one year and twelve days before the Japanese attack on Pearl Harbor. Chief was assigned to the Tenth Regiment of the United States Cavalry and he remained with the unit until the horse-mounted cavalry was officially disbanded in January 1950. At that time all horses 16 years of age or younger were sold by the Federal Government to private citizens. All older horses were retired to Fort Riley and were cared for by the Fort Riley Veterinary Service. At this time, Chief was 18 years old and he was consigned to live out his days under government care along with 222 other retirement-age horses. By the early 1960s, Chief was the only surviving horse. Because of his longevity, each year he attracted thousands of horse lovers to his small corral on the military post. The old cavalry veteran died in 1968 at the age of 36 and he was accorded a military funeral with all the corresponding honors and buried at the foot of the Old Trooper statue on the Cavalry Parade Field.

M113 ARMORED PERSONNEL CARRIER. Troopers from the First Battalion, Twenty-eighth Infantry, First Infantry Division exit from an M113 Armored Personnel during a training exercise in the 1970s. The M113 was designed to operate in conjunction with tanks delivering infantry squads to the battlefield. Troops exited by way of a ramp located at the back of the vehicle while a machine gunner located at the front gave covering fire.

SHERIDAN TANKS. Pictured are Sheridan Light Tanks from Fort Riley test firing Shillelagh Missiles during Operation Reforger IV, Grafenwohr, Federal Republic of Germany in early 1973. These troopers of the First Squadron, Fourth Cavalry Regiment, First Infantry Division are scouting out suspected enemy positions during war games in Germany. Because of its speed and lightweight construction, the Sheridan Light Tank was issued to scouting and reconnaissance units. The tank was equipped with a novel armament system that could fire both the Shillelagh Missile and conventional ammunition, including HEAT-MP, White Phosphorus, and canister rounds. Unfortunately, the tank was not a complete success in the field as its aluminum construction made it extremely vulnerable to enemy cannon and missile fire.

TANKS ON THE PLAINS. A combined arms team of armor and infantry training is pictured on the Kansas Plains in the mid-1980s. These units of the First Infantry division practiced combat maneuvers year round on Fort Riley's 100,920 acres of land available for military use. Beginning in 1955, Fort Riley was home to the First Infantry Division. In 1965, however, the division was deployed to South Vietnam where it remained for four-and-a-half years, performing search and destroy missions and pacification of the countryside. The division returned to the United States in April 1970 and remained on post until it returned to Wuerzburg, Germany in 1996.

REDEPLOYMENT. In the winter of 1973, the First Infantry Division took part in a massive redeployment from Fort Riley to the Federal Republic of Germany. This maneuver demonstrated the United States' ability to redeploy large numbers of troops on short notice to counter any Soviet threat to a NATO ally. Operation Reforger IV was a two-division, five-day exercise that involved the 6,923 troops of the First Infantry Division being airlifted to Germany. In this picture, troopers of A company, First Battalion, Sixty-Third Armor clean the 105mm rifled gun of their M60A3 tank that was propositioned in Germany for the exercise.

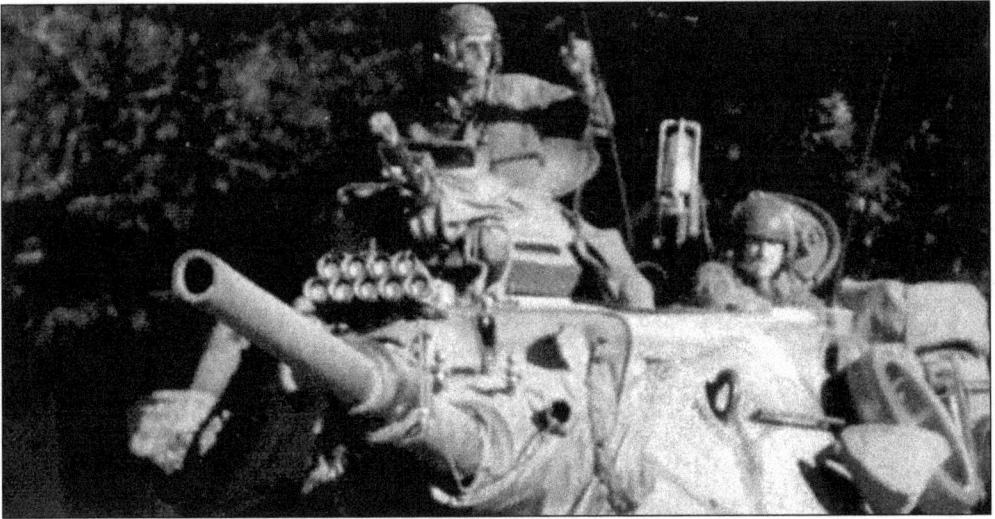

M60A3 MAIN BATTLE TANK. An M60A3 Main Battle Tank of the Sixty-Third Armor, First Infantry Division is shown here maneuvering on the open prairie, north of the main post. In the 1970s, the M60 tank was the principle main battle tank in the United States arsenal. This tank had served with American armored forces since 1960. Since that time, the tank had undergone significant modifications, including an upgraded 105mm main gun, an improved fire control system, a laser range finder, and a thermal sight. Even with these substantial improvements, by the 1970s the Army was searching for a replacement armored vehicle that would carry American tankers into the next century. As a result, the M1A1 replaced the M60. By 1980, these new tanks began to roll off the assembly line. The M1A1 Main Battle Tank acquitted itself well during the 1991 Gulf War, becoming the standard for the world's tanks.

IRWIN ARMY HOSPITAL AND CAMP WHITSIDE. This is an aerial view of Fort Riley Hospital and the Camp Whitside area, c.1970s. The Irwin Army Community Hospital opened in February 1958 and served the soldiers, dependents, and veterans of the Fort Riley community. The hospital was located in the Camp Whitside vicinity, which can be seen in the right-hand portion of the photograph. The hospital, named after Brigadier General Bernard John Dowling Irwin, "the Fighting Doctor," who won the Congressional Medal of Honor while fighting Chiricahua Indians in 1861.

CUSTER HILL. In 1966, Fort Riley added 66,000 acres to the military post. Coincidental with the land expansion was a large-scale building program west of the main post on Custer Hill. In the 1970s, facilities on Custer Hill were expanded to include vehicle repair shops, officer and enlisted personnel housing, and recreational facilities.

OLD BILL. Probably no other image captures the spirit of the United States Horse Cavalry than Frederick Remington's depiction of a grizzled cavalry veteran. Remington received his inspiration from an old trooper sergeant who was sitting on his horse in Tampa, Florida waiting to embark for combat in Cuba during the Spanish American War. The sergeant, who had enlisted under the name John Lannen, was in reality William Carrol, a Canadian immigrant. Lannen was a career soldier who had seen action on the American frontier. Remington believed that this noncommissioned officer represented the embodiment of the American horse trooper. Thousands of cavalrymen apparently agree with Remington's assessment, as "Old Bill" has symbolized the United States Cavalry since 1903.

Seven

THE SPORTING LIFE
OF RILEY

1920S ARMY HORSE SHOW TEAM. Horse shows, races, and polo matches resulted in the awarding of silver trophies and goblets to officers and enlisted men who participated. These officers, part of the Army Horse Show Team from the 1920s, proudly display their trophies.

1890s Baseball Team. In the last decade of the 19th century, baseball had become America's national pastime. Soldiers in the Army, like thousands of other Americans around the country, formed teams and played competitive baseball. Often the teams were formed from members of a particular unit, which encouraged friendly rivalry and healthy competition. Pictured here are the 1911 Fort Riley Post Baseball Champions of the Sixth Field Artillery.

1912 Baseball Team. 1912 Fort Riley Baseball Team, D Troop, Thirteenth Cavalry.

ARTILLERY BASEBALL TEAM. Players of the Artillery Baseball team are seen in 1936. Their stockings were red to denote the artillery branch color.

FIELD ARTILLERY FOOTBALL TEAM. Pictured are members of Battery A, Second Field Artillery's football team.

1897 Football Team. Football was another sport that captured America's imagination at the turn of the century. The Army encouraged the rough and tumble action of football, believing that the bruising competition toughened the men to the rigors of campaign life. In this picture, the men of the 1897 Battery A Second Field Artillery Football Team are shown. The crossed cannons on their jerseys denote their membership in the artillery branch.

Ninth Engineers Football Team. A photo of the Ninth Engineers football team, c. 1935. Note the man seated in the middle of the front row. It appears that he is wearing an early form of shoulder pads. None of the other men pictured seem to have this sort of protective equipment.

114

EQUESTRIAN SPORT. Troopers on a cavalry post favored equestrian sports. Steeplechases, endurance riding, and races were always popular attractions. During the interwar years, officers and enlisted alike engaged in equestrian activities that kept them and their horses in top condition. Here, a number of cavalrymen jump a water obstacle.

POLO. Polo was another popular equestrian sport among cavalrymen. Many of the post's officers played polo and fielded teams that competed against both army teams and civilian teams. United States Army Cavalry teams practiced and played hard, always hoping to win the coveted All Army Polo Team Trophy. This picture, taken during the interwar period, shows one of Fort Riley's many teams as it takes a break on the practice field.

JACKIE ROBINSON. Baseball great Jackie Robinson, the first African-American player to play major league baseball, served at Fort Riley during the early years of World War II. Here, Robinson is pictured on his mount in the stable area of Fort Riley's main post.

JOE LOUIS. Another giant of the sports world that served at Fort Riley during the World War II years was heavyweight boxing champion, Joe Louis. In this picture, Louis is carrying the national colors as the Eighth Training Field Squadron passes in review.

Eight

FORT RILEY
PERSONALITIES

BENNETT RILEY. Bennett Riley was born on November 27, 1787 in St. Mary's County, Maryland. A shoemaker by trade, Riley enlisted in the army at the age of 16 and was commissioned as Ensign in the Rifles, an elite corps, and fought in several engagements along the New York and Canadian border. After the war, the young officer was assigned to the American frontier where he battled the Arikara Indians in the Dakotas. In the spring of 1829, Riley led the first United States Army expedition to escort merchants traveling along the Santa Fe Trail. In the mid 1830s, Riley again saw action against Indians in both the Black Hawk War in Illinois and Wisconsin, and the Seminoles in Florida. During the Mexican War, he commanded the Second Infantry Regiment. For gallantry at the battles of Cerro Gordo and Contteras, Riley was promoted to the rank of brevet Major General. Following the war, he held commands in Louisiana and Missouri. In 1848, Riley was appointed commander of the Department of the Pacific, becoming the last military governor of California. As a result of this assignment, Riley assisted in crafting the state's constitution. In 1850, Riley was ordered to command the First Infantry Regiment, but was unable to assume the position because of illness. He died in Buffalo, New York in the late spring of 1853.

EDMUND A. OGDEN. Edmund A. Ogden was a native New Yorker who attended the United States Military Academy, graduating in 1833. Attached to the Quartermasters Corps, Ogden was assigned to various supply and construction related duties. In 1855, Major Ogden received orders to oversee the construction of permanent facilities at Fort Riley. One contemporary said that Ogden, "on horseback or on foot, was conspicuous for his general supervision of everything, ready to call attention to any neglect of work that did not seem to be going to the best advantage, and in that one month of July, I learned more than I ever have during the same length of time." Ogden, however, did not live to see his task completed, as the cholera epidemic that swept through Kansas in August 1855 claimed his life.

LEWIS ADDISON ARMISTEAD. Lewis Addison Armistead was born in 1817 and was related to George Armistead, the hero of Fort McHenry during the War of 1812. The young Armistead entered the United States Military Academy at West Point intending to follow his famous uncle's example, but left the institution before graduating. In July of 1839, Armistead became a second lieutenant and served with distinction during the Mexican War. Promoted to a captain in 1855, he was posted to frontier duty and was assigned to Fort Riley. When the Civil War began in 1861, Armistead offered his services to the Confederacy. He rose quickly and was soon promoted to brigadier general in Lee's Army of Northern Virginia. Armistead lost his life in July 1863, while participating in Pickett's Charge on the last day of the Battle of Gettysburg.

JOHN BUFORD. John Buford was born in Woodford, Kentucky on March 4, 1826. Appointed to the United States Military Academy at West Point, Buford graduated in 1848, receiving a commission as a second lieutenant in the First Dragoons. In the mid-1850s, Buford, then serving with the Second Dragoons, saw action against the Sioux Indians under Chief Little Thunder at Blue Water, Kansas. During this same period, Buford also assisted in putting down civil disturbances between Northern and Southern agitators in the Kansas Territory. In 1861, Buford returned east and one year later became a brigadier general, commanding a brigade of Union Cavalry in the Army of the Potomac. On the first day of the Battle of Gettysburg, Buford and his brigade distinguished themselves by delaying the advance of Robert E. Lee's army. Just a few months after the battle, Buford, who had been promoted to major general, became sick and died of typhoid fever.

ROBERT E. LEE. Robert E. Lee, the famous Confederate leader, spent a short time at Fort Riley in the autumn of 1855. Lee, who had just left an administrative position as Commandant of the United States Military Academy, was assigned to the United States Cavalry. As he was the ranking officer at Jefferson Barracks, Missouri, it was Lee's duty to tour frontier outposts and preside at various courts martial. In September 1855, Lee was sent to Fort Riley to sit in judgment on a case that involved an Army surgeon who had deserted his post during a particularly virulent epidemic. During the epidemic, 59 lives were claimed, including the wife of Captain Lewis Armistead, who would later command a brigade in Lee's Confederate Army of Northern Virginia.

JAMES EWELL BROWN STUART. James Ewell Brown Stuart was another notable Civil War cavalry commander. Stuart, a Virginian, attended the United States Military Academy and graduated in 1854. Commissioned in the Mounted Rifles, Stuart transferred to the First Regiment of Cavalry posted at Fort Riley, Kansas. During his time on the frontier he saw extensive action and was wounded while campaigning against the Cheyenne. In 1859, Stuart returned to the east and served as an aide to Robert E. Lee. In April of 1861, Stuart joined the Confederate Army, quickly becoming commander of Lee's cavalry. Stuart was responsible for a series of daring raids against the Union's Army of the Potomac. Stuart was killed in 1864 at the Battle of Yellow Tavern, while trying to blunt Ulysses S. Grant's drive against Richmond, Virginia.

GEORGE ARMSTRONG CUSTER. One of the most famous residents of Fort Riley was Lieutenant Colonel George Armstrong Custer. Custer, a native of Michigan and a graduate of the United States Military Academy, West Point, gained fame as a cavalry commander during the Civil War. Flamboyant and vain, he was, nonetheless, a competent and aggressive leader. During the Civil War, the young officer commanded the Michigan Cavalry Brigade, "the Wolverines." After the war, Custer remained in the cavalry and was sent West to police the frontier. As Commander of the Seventh Cavalry Regiment, Custer fought Indians primarily in Kansas, South Dakota, and Montana. He and a great portion of his command were wiped out by a combined force of Cheyenne and Sioux at the Battle of the Little Big Horn in June 1876.

GALUSHA PENNYPACKER. Even though the name Galusha Pennypacker may not be familiar to many students of America's frontier army, his name was noteworthy to his contemporaries. Pennypacker was born in Pennsylvania and served with gallant distinction during the Civil War. Wounded on seven different occasions during the conflict, the United States Congress honored his bravery by offering him a colonelcy in the Regulars at the conclusion of the war. Pennypacker served as commander of the Sixteenth United States Infantry when the unit was assigned to Fort Riley between 1877 and 1880. This distinguished officer ended his military career as the youngest general officer ever.

THOMAS BARRY. Thomas Barry, a Canadian and an Episcopalian pastor, was the Fort Riley Post Chaplain when the cornerstone was laid for St. Mary's Chapel in June of 1897. Barry was first appointed chaplain for Fort Leavenworth, Kansas in 1882 where he served in that capacity until 1889. After various assignments at Fort Sully, South Dakota; Fort Omaha, Nebraska; and Fort Snelling, Montana, Barry was posted to Fort Riley in 1894. He continued his military career by serving as chaplain for the artillery at Fort Monroe, Virginia. He died at Fort Monroe on February 24, 1904.

JAMES W. FORSYTH. James W. Forsyth was born in Ohio in 1838. He graduated from the United States Military Academy in 1851. Forsyth served on Major General George McClellan's staff during the early war years. Later in the war, he became Chief of Staff for Major General Philip Sheridan. After the Civil War, Forsyth moved west and fought Indians on the Great Plains. In 1887, he became commandant of Fort Riley, where he formulated a system of cavalry instruction that lasted until the horse cavalry disbanded in the early 1950s. In the early 1890s, Forsyth commanded the famed Seventh Cavalry during the Wounded Knee Campaign, which effectively ended the Indian Wars in the American West. He retired in the spring of 1897 and died in October 1906 at the age of 72.

GEORGE S. PATTON. George S. Patton, pictured here as a colonel in World War I. It can be argued that George S. Patton, alongside George Armstrong Custer, was one of the most colorful figures to grace the Cavalry Parade Field of Fort Riley. Patton, a 1909 graduate of the United States Military Academy, West Point, was posted to Fort Riley as a cavalry lieutenant just after his commissioning. Here the young officer was instrumental in developing the last cavalry saber adopted by the cavalry. As a versatile athlete, Patton represented the United States Army in the Pentathlon at the 1912 Stockholm Olympics. Patton saw action during Pershing's Punitive Expedition to Mexico in 1916, and in World War I he commanded the first tank brigade formed by the United States Army. His fame during World War II was legendary, leading United States forces in North Africa, Sicily, and Western Europe. Unfortunately, Patton's military career was cut short when he died of injuries suffered in a traffic accident in late 1945.

MALIN CRAIG. Major General Malin Craig, Chief of the Cavalry from 1924 to 1926. Craig was born on August 5, 1875 in St. Joseph, Missouri. He came from a long line of military men. His grandfather was a brigadier general of volunteers in the Union Army during the Civil War and his father was a 1874 graduate of West Point who fought in the Indian Wars. Like his father, he was also a graduate of the United States Military Academy and fought alongside his father in the Spanish American War. After the war, he transferred to the cavalry. During World War I, Craig served as Chief of Staff of the Forty-first Division. In 1921, he was a brigadier general and Commandant of the Cavalry School at Fort Riley. Promoted to Major General in 1924, Craig became Chief of Cavalry, a position he retained until 1926. In 1930, he was assigned to command the IX Area, a position he held until 1935. Craig received his fourth star in 1939 and became Chief of Staff of the Army. During his tenure as Chief of Staff, he reequipped the Army and initiated a program of tactical reorganization. Craig retired that same year but returned to duty in 1941. He died on July 22, 1945 after an extended illness.

HENRY "HAP" ARNOLD. Henry Harley Arnold, the "Father of the Modern United States Air Force," was born June 25, 1886 in Gladwyne, Pennsylvania, and attended the United States Military Academy. Graduating in 1903, Arnold served in the infantry branch until 1911 when he volunteered in the Army's program of flight training under the guidance of the Wright Brothers. He became one of the army's first aviators. In 1916, he was promoted to captain and assigned to the Aviation School at Rockwell Field, North Island, San Diego, California. During World War I, Arnold became assistant director of the military's program for training pilots. His postwar defense of General William (Billy) Mitchell earned him the reproach of the army and Arnold was "exiled" to Marshall Field, Fort Riley. By the early 1930s, the value of airpower was being reassessed by America's military and Arnold was rehabilitated. During World War II, Arnold, an advocate of strategic bombing, led America's air campaign against the Axis. Arnold died in Sonoma, California on January 15, 1950.

JONATHAN M. WAINWRIGHT. Jonathan M. Wainwright, the Hero of the Philippines and Corregidor, was born in Walla Walla, Washington in 1883. Wainwright attended the United States Military Academy, West Point, and graduated in 1906 as a second lieutenant in the cavalry. After seeing action fighting rebellious Moros in the Philippines and serving with the United States Expeditionary Force in France during World War I, he returned to Fort Riley, serving as both a student and instructor at the Cavalry School. From 1934 to 1936, Wainwright was Assistant Commandant of the Cavalry School. In 1940, he returned to the Philippines to command the United States forces Philippine Division. After the Japanese invasion of the islands in December 1941, he brilliantly battled the enemy until overwhelmed. Wainwright survived more than three years of captivity and was freed in time to witness the Japanese surrender on the USS Missouri. Wainwright died in September 1952 at Fort Sam Houston, Texas.

LUCIAN KING TRUSCOTT. Lucian King Truscott was not a West Point graduate. During World War I, he enlisted in the United States Army and was sent to Officers Candidate School where he was commissioned as a second lieutenant in the cavalry. After the war, he rose in the ranks serving in both Hawaii and in western Arizona. In the mid 1920s, Truscott was assigned to the Cavalry School at Fort Riley. He graduated from the school in 1926 and remained at the post as an instructor for the next five years. Throughout the 1930s, Truscott served with various cavalry and armored commands. When America entered World War II in 1941, he was sent to Europe to observe British military training, gaining valuable insight on their combat methods. In November 1942, Truscott became a divisional commander and served under Patton in North Africa and Sicily. Promoted to Corps Commander in 1944, he served in this capacity in both Italy and France. In late 1945, Truscott succeeded Patton in commanding the United States Third Army in the occupation of southern Germany. Truscott retired from the army in 1947 and died in Washington, D.C. in September 1965.

INNIS P. SWIFT. Innis P. Swift was born in Wyoming in February 1882. He attended the United States Military Academy and graduated with the Class of 1904. Swift served in the Philippines during the Moro Uprising, in Mexico with Pershing's Punitive Expedition, and with the Eighty-Second Infantry Division during World War I. In the early 1920s, Swift attended the Advanced Course of the Cavalry School at Fort Riley, Kansas. During those years at Fort Riley, colleagues remember him as a fine horsemen and an excellent polo player. In the early 1940s, Swift served as the Commanding General of the First Cavalry Division. He took part in the Louisiana Maneuvers of 1941 and at the outset of World War II he was sent to the Southwest Pacific. Swift was instrumental in the fighting that recaptured the Admiralty Islands and later commanded forces that returned to the Philippines under General Douglas MacArthur. It is worth noting that Swift's First Cavalry Division helped liberate Manila, the capital of the Philippines. He retired from the army in 1946 and died in San Antonio, Texas in November 1953.

JOHN (ANDY) SEITZ. John Seitz was a Kansas native who attended the University of Kansas from 1927 to 1930. He received a commission in the infantry but within a year transferred to the artillery branch. Between the years of 1933 and 1940, Sietz served in various postings. At the beginning of World War II he was assigned to Washington, D.C. as Executive Office, Pacific Section, Operations Division, War Department General Staff. For most of the war, he remained at this post. In December 1944, Seitz was transferred to Fort Shafter, Hawaii as Assistant Deputy Chief of Staff, Pacific Ocean Area. In the postwar years he held numerous postings around the globe including the Persian Gulf, Augsburg, Germany, and Washington, D.C. In February 1957, Seitz was ordered to Fort Riley, Kansas where he was assigned to command the artillery of the First Infantry Division. He retired from the Army in 1967 and died at the age of 78 in Junction City, Kansas.

GORDON RUSSELL SULLIVAN. Gordon Russell Sullivan was born in September 1937 in Boston, Massachusetts. He graduated from Norwich University, Northfield, Vermont with a degree in history. Sullivan has held various assignments including postings in Vietnam, Korea, and Germany. In the late 1960s, he attended the Army Command and General Staff College, Fort Leavenworth, Kansas. Sullivan was promoted to brigadier general in 1984 and major general in 1987. He became Commander of the First Infantry Division at Fort Riley in 1988, a post he held until July 1989. In 1990, he was made Vice Chief of Staff, Office of the Chief of Staff United States Army, Washington, D.C.

CARL VUONO. Carl Edward Vuono was born in Monongahela, Pennsylvania, on October 18, 1934. He attended the United States Military Academy and graduated in 1960. Commissioned in the artillery, he served with the 3rd Armored Cavalry and 1st Cavalry Division. He served two tours in Vietnam, one with the 1st Infantry Division. Vuono's service with the Big Red One continued when he was assigned as the assistant division commander at Fort Riley from 1977 through 1979. He capped his career by becoming the chief of staff of the Army in 1987—a post he held until his retirement in 1991. General Vuono now resides in the Washington, D.C. area.

JAMES HILLIARD POLK. James Hilliard Polk was born of Army parents at Batangas, Philippine Islands on December 13, 1911. He graduated from the United States Military Academy, West Point, New York in June 1933. Polk was commissioned in the United States Cavalry and served with that branch of service in a variety of posts, which included Fort Bliss, Texas; West Point, New York; Fort Riley, Kansas; and Fort Leavenworth, Kansas. During World War II, he served in the European Theater of Operations commanding the Sixth Cavalry Group Mechanized and the Third Cavalry Group Mechanized. At this time Polk was decorated three times for gallantry, once by General George Patton. After the war, he served as Chief of Tactics at the Ground General School, Fort Riley, Kansas. When the Korean War broke out he was transferred to the Far East serving on the staff of General Douglas MacArthur. During the Cold War, Polk held many diplomatic and military posts. He retired a General in 1971, and died in 1992.

Visit us at
arcadiapublishing.com

www.ingramcontent.com/pod-product-compliance
Lightning Source LLC
Chambersburg PA
CBHW050653150426
42813CB00055B/1684

9 781531 617684